God's Profound

and

URGENT MESSAGE

God will not force His will on you. You are free to choose.
But you are not free to choose the consequences of your choice.

A Compassionate Call to Hear God's Message

God's Profound *and* URGENT MESSAGE

God will not force His will on you. You are free to choose.
But you are not free to choose the consequences of your choice.

MIKE G. NORTON

A Compassionate Call to Hear God's Message

REDEMPTION
PRESS

Published by Redemption Press, PO Box 427, Enumclaw, WA 98022

Toll Free (844) 2REDEEM (273-3336)

Redemption Press is honored to present this title in partnership with the author. The views expressed or implied in this work are those of the author. Redemption Press provides our imprint seal representing design excellence, creative content, and high quality production.

All emphasis (italics) in Scriptures has been added by the author.

In an effort to keep to the center of interest I have not always quoted the *entire* verse, but rather focused on the phrase that was appropriate just as Jesus and the apostles often did to make a point.

ISBN 13: 978-1-68314-335-2

Library of Congress Catalog Card Number: 2017944118

Presented to

From

Date

Contents

Part 3

God's Primary Message to Mankind: "Listen to My Instruction"

Part 4

Jesus Christ, His Absolute Authority, and the Only Source of Salvation

Part 5

God's Loving Promises to Believers

Part 6

Sin, Separation, Prayer, and God's Forgiveness

Part 7

False Religions, Varied Teachings, and the Consequence of Unbelief

Part 8

Christ's Return and His Divine Message to Mankind

Acknowledgments

For His Glory
To the righteousness and abounding love and mercy
of our God and Savior Jesus Christ,
Thank You
for answered prayer,
for help, guidance, and content.
This book and the driving force of its message
were accomplished by the grace and will of God.

- I am grateful to God for the special people at REDEMPTION PRESS, whose support, guidance, professional editing and graphic design far exceeded what I expected, and with special thanks to Hannah McKenzie, Maryna Zhukov, Barbara Kois, Niki Manbeck and Nate Myers.
- I am also grateful to God for our special church family, my family, my sisters and my dear wife Michelle.
- I am most grateful to God and have an infinite debt of gratitude for all He did for us, and for preserving as He promised, the divine record the Bible, and for making known the gospel of Christ and way to eternal salvation.

Introduction

Dear Friend,

From the very beginning, I want to make clear that it is vitally important that this book be *true to Scripture*, as the Bible states: "If anyone speaks, they should do so as one who speaks the very words of God" (1 Peter 4:11 NIV). Therefore, throughout this book, both the Scriptural verse *and* the biblical source will be referenced and identified. This is not a daily devotional book or a book of ideas or opinions from man, religion, or the author. It is far more important. It is Scriptural wisdom, truth, and instruction from the Word of God to man.

If you are about to read this book, I assure you, just surely as you are breathing air right now, you have God's light shining on you. How blessed you are! This book is dedicated to *you*. God has predestined this very time in your life and it is by no accident you are holding and reading this book. Know that regardless of your religious beliefs, present or past situation, God has great eternal plans and magnificent promises He wants to share with you. God will be revealing life-saving information to you here. Read it carefully, share it, and pass it on. Each truth God reveals is a pearl of great value and a magnificent promise.

God longs for the loving intimacy of a friend; that we come closer to Him, knowing Him, trusting Him, believing in Him. All down through the ages, too many people have become dependent upon man and religion for the source of "truth and guidance" to salvation, rather than the Word of God, and in doing so, some have grievously erred. Why? Because not all religions represent "truth" and the God of our Bible. God is calling on all of us to come to Him, talk to Him, listen to Him, and then we will truly know *God's* way and "truth."

Seek God's Word from Scripture and the message of truth He is conveying. Meditate on it. Ponder it. Delight in it. Not to draw your own conclusions, but to be absorbed in *His*. Such truth is like a rope passed to a drowning man, and every truth, every pull is one pull closer to shore, to safety, to God. Remember that illustration. Hold on to the rope, to the words of our Lord, and affirm them. *Genuine* faith and trust are the *key* that unlocks the storehouse of God's resources. You carry out His wishes and abide in His Word, and He will give you clearer and more definite teaching and guidance.

Do not entertain thoughts of doubt and disbelief about God and His message from the media, worldly scholars, or secular teachers and professors. Never tolerate them even for a second. Lock the doors and bar the windows of your soul against them as you would with your home against a robber who would steal your treasures and harm your family. Those who know God would never think God wishes to harm them.

At this moment, God is still granting us time and mercy and patience, but this is running out. God is pleading with all nations and all people of the earth to draw near to Him, hear Him, and listen to Him. God wants the world to understand and recognize the indisputable evidence and reasons for the credibility and accuracy of the Bible and why it should be adhered to, and to understand His most profound and dominant messages with a due sense of *urgency* for salvation. Therefore, this book will carefully address these and other issues, and as stated earlier, identify the verse and biblical source of each quote where necessary.

The primary intent of this book is sixfold: To give Scriptural evidence of:

1. The Scriptural and external evidence of the credibility and accuracy of the Bible.
2. The fact that God personally knows and dearly loves you.
3. God longs for you to know Him, to trust Him, and to believe in Him.
4. God's truly "precious and magnificent promises."
5. Jesus Christ's absolute authority and God's true way, leading to eternal salvation.
6. The importance of recognizing the dangers of deception, perverse and varied teachings, and the consequence of sin and unbelief.

This book is a valuable reference tool for quickly discovering what was said concerning the above-mentioned issues, our lives, and more. You will learn the Lord's message and the answers to many important questions in an easy-to-understand, accurate, and powerful format. Know the truth (of the questions) and the will of God.

As you read each question and answer, please, go s-l-o-w-l-y and allow God's loving words from Scripture to sink in to fully grasp its entirety, the steps, the scope, the width and depth, and the eternal value each Scriptural message is conveying. These are His inspired words from the Bible and they convey the insights into the mind and heart of our loving God. Listen carefully to His message, eagerly, joyfully. Don't crowd it out! Take your time. Mark or highlight the statements that focus on issues of importance.

This is no ordinary book. It holds in part the Word and will of God. It is a mine of spiritual treasures to share with all. Christianity is a loving relationship with our God. The primary intent of this book is to provide the factual evidence of biblical credibility, and the reasons and steps for believing and living as God wants. The Bible provides the plan for salvation and bringing redemption and restoration to our country through the family and church, in a worldwide culture bent on pushing God out of our lives, our schools, our government, and our courts.

Know that God is inviting you personally, right now, today, to hear His loving message and to participate in the greatest, largest, and most diverse and significant cause in history: His kingdom. God says: "I will instruct you and teach you in the way which you should go; I will counsel you with My eye upon you" (Ps. 32:8 NASB). "For I am the Lord, your God, who takes hold of your right hand and says to you, Do not fear; I will help you" (Isa. 41:13 NIV).

Nothing else you do in this life will matter as much as establishing and maintaining a relationship with God and sharing with others how they can have eternal life. I know personally the transforming power of the Word of God for those who believe.

God is calling on all of us saying; "Come to me, all you who labor and are heavy laden, and I will give you rest. Take my yoke upon you, and learn from Me, for I am gentle and lowly in heart, and you will find rest for your souls. For my yoke is easy, and my burden is light" (Matt. 11:28-30 ESV). "I want you to understand what *really* matters, so that you may live pure and blameless lives until the day of Christ's return" (Phil. 1:10 NLT). God is calling on all of us to come to *Him* and learn from *Him*. Scripture says: "The eyes of the Lord search the whole earth in order to strengthen those whose hearts are fully committed to Him" (2 Chron. 16:9 NLT).

You cannot see what the future holds but don't fear because God can, and He knows better than you what you need. Trust Him absolutely. Trust His every word. You are not at the mercy of fate or man. You are being led in a very definite way, and others who do not serve your purpose are being moved out of your path by God. Know that God is inviting you, leading you, and His loving grace is on you. His Word is your source of wisdom. Know that nothing here is by chance.

God is pleading that we all individually and as a nation, come to know the truth, by coming to know Him and His Word, the Bible, while there still remains time and mercy. "Turn to Me and be saved, all the ends of the earth; For I am God, and there is no other" (Isa. 45:22 NASB). "For I know the plans I have for you, says the Eternal, plans for peace, not evil, to give you a future and hope, never forget that" (Jer. 29:11 VOICE). The greatest eternal blessings await all those who sincerely welcome and read God's message and believe and abide in His Word, and let the reader see for himself, if God will not open for *you*, the door to wisdom, understanding and the truth of our *creators will* and way to salvation.

The Use of Many Bible Translations

The intentional use of varied Bible translations in this book provides subtle distinctions, variations, and shades of meaning that can easily be missed using only one Bible, so it is always helpful to compare translations. Therefore, different Bible translations including paraphrases, were used to help see God's truth and promises more easily and clearly, while accurately conveying the critical message. Furthermore, we can sometimes miss the full impact of certain Bible verses simply because they become so familiar that we just "pass over" their meaning or significance. As you read this book use a yellow marker to highlight important issues to be remembered.

Produced for: Your personal benefit, and to help you understand the eternal value and magnificent promises of knowing and complying with God's loving message.

This book is: Dedicated to you! Before you were born, God planned this moment in your life. It is by no accident you are reading this book. "For the Son of Man has come to seek and to save that which was lost" (Luke 19:10 NASB).

God's message: "Be still, and know that I *am* God" (Psalm 46:10 NKJV). "All you nations, come near and listen. Pay attention. The earth and all the people in it should listen" (Isa. 34:1 NCV). God is *pleading* for your attention. "Listen, O my people, to My instruction, incline your ears to the words of My mouth" (Ps. 78:1 NASB). "For I want you to understand what really matters" (Phil. 1:10 NLT). This is a book on Bible doctrine, on God's profound and urgent message to mankind.

Test this book: The apostle Paul said, "But examine everything carefully; hold fast to that which is good" (1 Thess. 5:21 NASB). "Don't despise what God has revealed" (1 Thess. 5:20 GW). "He who believes in Me, as the Scripture has said, out of his heart will flow rivers of living water" (John 7:38 NKJV).

With God's help, make the most of this book

Understand that anyone can read God's inspired message in Scripture; however, without the illumination of the Holy Spirit it won't make sense to him. As Scripture says, "But people who aren't spiritual can't receive these truths from God's Spirit. It all sounds foolish to them and they can't understand it, for only those who are spiritual can understand what the Spirit means" (1 Cor. 2:14 NLT). "For the message of the cross is foolish to those who are perishing, but to us who are being saved it is the Power of God" (1 Cor. 1:18 NKJV).

Therefore, before you begin . . .

Pray and *earnestly ask* that God may reveal His will to *you*.

Know this: God explicitly says: "Call unto Me, and I will answer thee" (Jer. 33:3 KJV).

"Teach me, O Lord, the way of Your statutes . . . Give me understanding, that I may observe Your law . . . Make me walk in the path of Your commandments . . . Incline my heart to Your testimonies . . . And revive me in Your ways, Establish Your Word to Your servant, As that which produces reverence for You" (Ps. 119:33-38 NASB).

"I pray that the eyes of my heart may be enlightened, So that I may know what is the hope of your calling. And what is the surpassing greatness of your power towards those who believe" (Eph. 1:18-19 author paraphrase). "Strengthen me according to Your Word, Amen" (Ps. 119:28 NKJV). "Now may the God of hope fill you with all joy and peace in believing, so that you will abound in hope by the power of the Holy Spirit" (Rom. 15:13 NASB).

PART 1

The Facts About the Bible

CHAPTER 1

The Indisputable Evidence, Credibility, and Accuracy of the Bible

Stop and think! Would a creator, having supreme intelligence, wisdom, and the love to think out, plan, design, and bring about all creation, then leave His created beings in complete ignorance of Him and His laws? God almighty did not hide these important truths from human minds, but made them accessible in the Holy Bible, His instruction book for mankind. The oneness or unity of the Bible is a miracle. It is a library of sixty-six books, written by forty different authors, over a time span of approximately 1,600 years, and dating back from 1500 BC to about 100 years after Christ.

The Bible was originally written in three different ancient languages. It was written in Hebrew, Aramaic, and Greek. Represented in the authors is a cross-section of humanity, educated and uneducated, including kings, fishermen, public officials, farmers, teachers, and physicians. Included in the subjects are religion, history, law, science, poetry, drama, biography, and prophecy. Yet all the various parts are as harmoniously *united* as the parts that make up the human body! For forty different authors with such varied backgrounds to write on so many subjects, in three different languages over such a long period of approximately 1,600 years, in absolute harmony, is a mathematical impossibility. It just could not have happened!

How then do we account for the Bible? Scripture states; "Every word we speak was taught to us by God's Spirit, not by human wisdom. And this same Spirit helps us teach spiritual things to spiritual people" (1 Cor. 2:13 CEV). The Bible says, "Understand this first: No part of the Holy Writings was ever made up by any man. No part of the Holy Writings came because of what man wanted to write. But holy men who belonged to God spoke what the Holy Spirit told them" (2 Peter 1:20-21 NLV).

Our Lord also revealed, "Now the man Moses was very humble, more than any man who was on the face of the earth" (Num. 12:3 NASB). "It is different when I speak with my servant Moses; I have put him in charge of all my people Israel. So I speak to him [Moses] face-to-face, clearly . . . [directly], he has even seen my form!" (Num. 12:7-8 GNT). Moses was singled out as God's servant. He is described as uniquely close to the Lord, and his importance is underscored by our Lord's direct face-to-face communications with him. The fifth book of Moses, commonly called Deuteronomy, is so important that it's one of the books that's quoted most often by Jesus Himself and His apostles. There are over eighty references to this book in the New Testament. By way of reference, Jesus confirms the authority and credibility of his book in the Bible.

But God did not stop there. Historians usually admit that *greater* credibility must be granted to the very people who were both geographically and chronologically close to the events they were reporting. With that in mind, just look at the care God took when He inspired the writing of the New Testament. The overwhelming degree of scholarship confirms that the evidence and accounts of Jesus' life and His statements, together with the letters that form the bulk of the New Testament, were all written by men who were either eyewitnesses to the events they recorded or from other eyewitnesses.

God purposely selected Matthew, Mark, Luke, and John to write the four gospels for a reason. These were persons who could say with authority such things as, "I saw all this myself and have given an accurate report so that you also can believe" (John 19:35 TLB). God could have used anyone anywhere to write His words about Jesus Christ.

However, to give us additional confidence and validity in the truth being recorded, God worked through *eyewitnesses* such as John, who said in Scripture, "Again I say, we are telling you about that which we ourselves have actually seen and heard" (1 John 1:3 TLB), or through Peter, an apostle, when he said, "But we were eyewitness of His majesty" (2 Peter 1:16 NASB) "and we ourselves heard this utterance made from heaven when we were with Him on the mountain" (2 Peter 1:18 NASB). These were eyewitnesses who had "seen and heard." Paul an apostle of Jesus Christ declared, "*Do not be mistaken*; our words come from God with the utmost sincerity, always spoken through the Anointed in the presence of God." "We speak the truth before God, as messengers of God" (2 Corin. 2:17 VOICE; NCV).

Most of Christ's apostles were eventually tortured and martyred for holding on to their testimony. Even to the point of death, Christ's apostles did not recant their story. This alone demonstrates that their testimony was true, as who would ever suffer torture and death for telling something false? But God still did not stop there, in validating and proving the special uniqueness of the Bible. Oh no, He went much further and added to it something no man can. It has hundreds of fulfilled prophecies that further authenticate God's special book from that of any other in the entire world. The Bible contains well over 1000 prophecies and God declared in Scripture that "No prophecy was ever made by an act of human will" (2 Peter 1:21 NASB). God had a powerful reason to make 25 percent of the Bible prophetic when it was first written. One of the strongest and most irrefutable arguments for the accuracy and credibility of the Bible is its 100 percent accuracy rate in predicting the future.

It proves beyond all doubt that He is God. Fulfilled prophecy is solid proof and the clearest evidence that demonstrates the Bible is absolutely supernatural and the inspiration of God. It is truly, God's Word. Even the Bible itself confirms this by stating 3,808 times the words, "Thus says the Lord . . . " or "God spoke . . . " or "The Lord said . . . " or "The Word of the Lord . . . " or "The Word of God. . . . "

If the Bible is not the Word of God, it has to be the biggest hoax and bundle of lies perpetrated by man on this planet. The Bible *is* the Word of God and the absolute truth because God cannot lie. God said, "Turn to Me and be saved, all the ends of the earth; for I am God, and there is no other. By Myself I have sworn, My mouth has uttered in all integrity the word that will not be revoked" (Isa. 45:22-23 NIV).

God is telling us that His mouth has spoken integrity and not a word will be revoked. Furthermore, when Scripture speaks, God speaks. Romans 3:2 AMP declares that the Scriptures are the oracles, the "very words" of God. We can trust His Word! The Bible has surely stood the test of time and towers well over all other authoritative books because of fulfilled prophecy. But while hundreds of fulfilled prophecies validates the Bible as a Divine inspired supernatural book to believed, it is much more! The remaining *unfilled* prophecies is also God's way of giving us fair warning, so we can prepare our hearts and minds to be ready for the events *coming ahead!* No Christian can afford to be ignorant of prophecy in these days which we live in because the things that are prophesied in God's Word are imminent. As the front cover of this book depicts, the sands of the hour glass are quickly running low and I believe we are standing on the threshold of the coming of Jesus Christ and the rapture of the church. (further explained later in this book) I believe there is no remaining biblical sign or prophecy that must take place before the rapture can happen. For the sake of family and loved ones we cannot afford to be ignorant of God's profound and urgent message in the Bible.

Furthermore, because of the redemptive and instructional purpose of the Bible, God cannot, and will not allow it to be destroyed, twisted, or distorted. As the Lord Himself said in reassuring us, "For truly, I say to you, until Heaven and earth pass away, not an iota, not a dot, will pass from the law until all is accomplished" (Matt. 5:18 ESV).   His teachings are not only authoritative ("For truly, I say to you"), they are also permanent.

God's will, *will prevail!* He will permit nothing to impede His purpose. As the Lord further declared, "Heaven and earth shall pass away, but My Words shall not pass away" (Matt. 24:35 KJV). "But the Word of the Lord endureth for ever" (1 Peter 1:25 KJV). Jesus clearly reveals that the permanence of God's Word extends to the smallest letters and the smallest parts of printed letters, and neither shall be erased or modified. No other statement by the Lord more clearly states, with such powerful and over whelming conviction, His absolute and total confidence in the enduring nature and inerrant flawless quality of the Bible. It is God's own Word down to every single word, letter and dot. In view of that reality, how foolish are we to ever wonder about the validity and relevancy of God's Word.

Furthermore, Jesus Himself stated, "The Scripture cannot be broken" (John 10:35 NASB). The Bible is God's eternal Word, and Scripture says, "In humility receive the Word implanted, which is able to save your souls" (James 1:21 NASB). In view of the above, and in considering our obligations to the divine Scripture as Christians, we must defend the Word of God. We should always strive for the integrity, authority, and purity of God's book, the Holy Bible.

Did you know that even historians agree to the authenticity of the Bible, and contrary to popular belief, transmission of the text was completed with 99.9 percent precision (determined by textual criticism and comparisons of thousands and thousands of existing manuscripts). God has not left us to wonder. He has miraculously supervised the transmission of His Word to ensure that it was relayed accurately from one generation to another. He said, "Write down these words. Write them in a book. They will stand until the end of time as a witness" (Isa. 30:8 NLT). On God's word, you can rest assured that we have His accurate Word as a witness today!

But God did not stop there in strengthening the textual evidence and reliability of His Word in the Bible. He worked to further reinforce the authenticity of the Scriptures. A routine criterion in examining and cross-checking historical documents is whether there exists "any other" historical material which confirms or disproves the testimony of the document in question. Historians ask "What 'other' sources apart from the literature under examination (in this case, the Bible) substantiate its accuracy and reliability?" In all of history, the Bible is, by far, the most widely referenced and quoted book. Did you know, the New Testament alone is so extensively quoted in the ancient manuscripts of non-biblical authors that all twenty-seven books, from Matthew through Revelation, could be reconstructed virtually word for word just from those sources. God's Word truly endureth forever and stands until the end of times.

God still did not stop there! Over 24,000 manuscripts or "fragments of manuscripts" of the New Testament repose in the universities and libraries of the world. There are presently 5,686 Greek manuscripts in existence today for the New Testament, which makes the New Testament the best-attested document in all ancient writings. All totaled, these manuscripts include more than two million pages of text. The number of manuscripts and pages is absolutely staggering and because there are so many, they can be cross-checked for accuracy. After minor spelling errors and variations in word order are taken out, they agree with one another more than 99 percent of the time. Of the remaining slight variants, there is nothing that would alter God's Word that would affect the Christian faith.

There's not even one difference that decisively affects any part of the Christian faith! As Scripture states, "Every word of God is flawless" (Prov. 30:5 NIV). With all the facts and evidence God has provided us about the Bible, He still did not stop there! He went even further to reassure us that His Word is true *even today!* He allowed the critically important and recent discovery of the Dead Sea Scrolls to prove it. The Dead Sea Scrolls are considered by many to be the single most important archaeological manuscript find of the twentieth century. Over 800 scrolls were identified in caves, just thirteen miles east of Jerusalem and 1300 feet below sea level between 1947 and 1956. In fact, the scrolls are the *oldest* group of Old Testament manuscripts ever found. One scroll found in Cave 11 measured 26.7 feet long, and the Isaiah Scroll was found relatively intact. Some of the larger ones originally stretch as long as thirty feet.

The most incredible discovery was the immense library of Biblical manuscripts found in Cave Four at Qumran. It contained every book of the Old Testament with the exception of the Book of Esther. There were also multiple copies of several biblical texts such as Genesis, Deuteronomy and Isaiah in Cave Four. As a result of this important discovery, scholars were able to reach far back in time to examine the ancient texts that had rested undisturbed in the desert caves for so many centuries.

What scholars discovered in their findings was that even though more than 1,000 years separated these very ancient Dead Sea Scrolls from what we did have (the Masoretic texts), the Dead Sea Scrolls and the Masoretic texts agreed word for word more than 95 percent of the time! The remaining differences were primarily due to minor spelling variations. These very ancient findings give further evidence that the Hebrew Scriptures we have today are remarkably true to the *original* writings. We can be confident that our Bible today is faithful to the original manuscripts and that the absolute truth, accuracy, and authority of the Scriptures stand firm today.

Even the very stones cry out that God's Word is true. Over and over again, the reliability and accuracy of the Bible have been regularly and consistently supported by archaeology. The biblical events, the cities and the people have *all* been historically verified. The extensive and external evidence for the Bible is an extremely rare phenomenon, and it makes the Holy Bible unique and unlike any other religious writings of the world.

It is truly amazing to see how the Word of God has traveled through the ages and languages and cultures. It began in the language of His chosen people, adopted the language of the Roman world, and now exists in over 2,000 different languages. Far from being static, that is, a single language text, the Bible actually embraces translations and cross-language accessibility by its very nature. Whether you read the Bible in its original language or in one of the thousands of modern languages, it's a blessing to be able to read God's Word today just as it was read thousands of years ago. As the Bible says, "The sum of Thy Word is Truth" (Ps. 119:160 NASB). The Bible is God's divine book to instruct and judge us; we are not here to judge the Bible or question God's almighty power and ability to preserve and maintain His Word forever, as He said He would. Since when is man, the creature whose mind is so *very limited*, to now be qualified enough to judge the Creator's work, since He has an infinite mind? Do not be influenced by people or religious organizations that discredit the teachings of Christ in the Bible.

The Bible is God's infallible Word and says of itself, "The Law of the Lord is Perfect, converting the soul: the testimony of the Lord is sure, making wise the simple" (Ps. 19:7 AKJV). The Bible is not only infallible in its totality but it is also *inerrant* in all its parts. Scripture declares: "Every word of God is flawless" (Prov. 30:5 NIV), and God's Word has eternal force! (see Isa. 55:11). Therefore, God's Word is free from error and absolutely trustworthy.

The combined and cumulative evidence for the accuracy and reliability of the Bible is not only convincing and compelling, but a clear indication of how God has supervised its preservation for us and our children, His loving message for salvation, and the many blessings that come from knowing, trusting, and abiding in His Word.

Therefore, the ultimate criterion for determining the importance and validity of anything pertaining to God, life, or salvation is the Holy Bible, and God's very character rests upon the *authenticity* and *authority* of the Bible. As Scripture says, "Heaven and earth shall pass away: but my words shall not pass away" (Mark 13:31 AKJV).

Do not be deceived. The Bible is the *only* rule of faith and practice that counts. You do not need religious books to study the Bible. The Bible *itself* is its own best commentary and explanation. God states that "The Scriptures were written to teach us and encourage us by giving us hope" (Rom. 15:4 CEV). God has included everything in the Bible that He wants you to know and that is necessary to know concerning salvation and your Christian life.

The Bible is God's instruction book and love letter to mankind. We are *commanded* to know it. Jesus said, "It is written, Man is not to live on bread only. Man is to live by every word that God speaks" (Matt. 4:4 NLT). "He should keep it with him all the time and read from it every day of his life. Then he will learn to respect the Lord his God, and he will obey all the teachings and commands" (Deut. 17:19 NCV). God's laws command supreme attention over and above *any* religious denomination, organization, government, or court, as no other entity in the world can provide you with eternal salvation.

Daily Bible reading will keep you in range of God's voice. Scripture commands, "Like newborn babies, crave the pure spiritual milk, so that by it you may grow up in your salvation" (1 Peter 2:2 NIV). Why?

Because spiritual growth, as you will discover, is the process of replacing misconception and lies with truth. Therefore, feeding on God's Word *must* be our first priority because it is one of God's greatest gifts to mankind, to lead him into the full, abundant life, to protect him, and to lead him into eternal life. All the evil in the world today is caused by disobedience of our Creator's laws.

Please, please take the time and take to heart the truth of God's statements herein. You do not want to leave your eternity to guesswork. If you are one who believes that if you lead a good life and do some good works you will end up in heaven, are you certain about your decision? If so, what do you base your certainty on?

No other book in the world, or other "written religious authority" in all of history, has provided such purity of text, such a degree of historical and archaeological confirmations, and such extensive prophecy fulfilled like the Bible does. It simply does not exist! God has given us the most historically reliable and accurate document in the world today—the Holy Bible. With it He is seeking our attention. Our part is to be attentive to His loving message.

CHAPTER 2

Has God Made It Known to Man that There Really Is a God? Yes.

"For what can be known about God is plain to them, because God has shown it to them" (Rom. 1:19 ESV). "For every home is built by someone, but the builder of all things is God" (Heb. 3:4 NASB). "For by Him all things were created, in heaven and on earth, visible and invisible, whether thrones or dominions or rulers or authorities, all things were created through Him and for Him" (Col. 1:16 ESV).

"God is the One who made all things, and all things are made for His glory" (Heb. 2:10 NCV). "Yes, God made all things and everything continues through Him and for Him" (Rom. 11:36 NCV). "The heavens are telling of the glory of God; And their expanse is declaring the work of His hands" (Ps. 19:1 NASB). "Who does great things, unfathomable, and wondrous works without number" (Job 9:10 NASB). "For since the creation of the world His invisible attributes, His eternal power and divine nature, have been clearly seen, being understood through what has been made, so that they are *without excuse*" (Rom. 1:20 NASB).

Comment: In all of creation, only human beings are made in God's image (See Gen. 1:27 NASB). This is a great privilege and gives us dignity.

The extreme precision and special requirements needed for sustaining life on earth are far too complex, and the vastness of the heavens are far too great to logically deny an intelligent design and a creator. Just as one would not deny there is a creator for a watch or a home, it would not be realistic to claim there is no creator for human life and all that exists.

God's message above conveys He is the Creator, and the evidence of "what has been made" proves it. In each of the coming chapter questions that follow, the answers are all from God's infallible book called the Bible. It is the Word of God and God's authoritative and declaring message to all of us. In it, He pleads, "Come here and listen, O nations of the earth. Let the world and everything in it hear My words" (Isa. 34:1 NLT).

As we age and find ourselves in our last years of life, we all realize that relationships are what life is all about. Wisdom is learning the truth sooner than later. Don't wait until you are on your deathbed to figure out what matters most, and that almighty God loves you and yearns to be your friend! He is a God who is passionate about His relationship with you (Exodus 34:14 NLT). Did you know He planned our world, including the details of our lives, so that we could become His friends? The Bible says, "Starting from scratch, God made the entire human race and made the earth hospitable, with plenty of time and space for living so we could seek after God, and not just grope in the dark but actually *find* Him" (Acts 17:27 MSG). Therefore, seek to know Him now because God does exist. As the Bible tells us, God's eternal power and divine nature have been *clearly* seen as evident by what has been made.

Part 1

Scriptural Summary Points to Remember

- The Bible never came by the will of man, but in words spoken by God and taught by the Holy Spirit. Every word of God is flawless.

- It was written over a period of approximately 1,600 years, dating from 1500 BC to about 100 years after Christ.

- No prophecy was ever made by an act of human will.

- Heaven and earth shall pass away but God's Word shall never pass away.

- The Scriptures are the oracles, the "very words" of God.

- God's words in Scripture will stand until the end of time.

- The Bible has a 100 percent accuracy rate in predicting the future.

- We need more than bread for life; we must feed on every word of God.

- Crave the pure milk of the Word to grow up in salvation.

- The heavens are telling of the glory of God, their expanse is declaring the work of His hands.

- For by Him all things were created.

- Since the creation of the world, God's divine nature and power have been clearly seen, being understood through *what has been made.*

- Come to *Me*, listen to *Me*. Let the world and everything in it hear *My* words.

- In humility receive the Word implanted which is able to save your souls.

- Don't despise what God has revealed.

- For I am God and there is no other. By myself I have sworn, My mouth has spoken integrity and not a word will be revoked.

PART 2

God Personally Knows and Loves You

CHAPTER 3

Does God Know Anything about You? Yes.

"I know *everything* about you" (Ps.139:1, Ps. 44:21, Jer.12:3 author paraphrase). "It is I who made the earth, and created man upon it. I stretched out the heavens with My hands, and I ordained all their host" (Isa. 45:12 NASB). "I am your Creator. You were in My care even before you were born" (Isa. 44:2 CEV). "Before I formed you in the womb, I knew you" (Jer. 1:5 ESV). "My eyes have seen you before you were formed. For all your days were written in My book, before any one of them came to be" (Ps. 139:16 author paraphrase).

As God explains in Isaiah 46:3 NCV: "I have carried you since you were born; I have taken care of you from your birth." "You were predestined before I planned creation" (Eph. 1:5, 11 author paraphrase). "I determined the exact pre-appointed time of your birth and where you would live" (Acts 17:26 author paraphrase). "Know that the Lord, He *is* God; It is He *who* has made us, and not we ourselves" (Ps. 100:3 NKJV).

Comment: There is no conclusive scientific evidence that man has come up from the ape, and we have not come about by chance or evolution. The whole theory of evolution holds that there is no God and that everything in the entire universe including all the complexities of life and the incredibly intricate genetic DNA code that contains a staggering amount of vital information, had all developed from nothing and by chance. However, the theory of evolution is falling apart today in the face of a total lack of evidence to support its hypothesis. The sheer complexity of life and the vast amounts of information required to sustain life are beyond imagination. Currently, biologists cannot even explain all the activities and workings going on inside the cell without comparing it to advanced and complex engineering. As they carefully observe the interior functions and operations of the human cell, it becomes very apparent there is a complexity and sophistication that's beyond the sphere of human technological innovation or comprehension.

The average human body has about 100 trillion cells and each one contains enough information to fill a one million page encyclopedia, which is used to control the functions of the human body. Do consider it! The sequential order of the letters in DNA determines the structure of a human being down to his slightest details. In addition to features like height, eye, hair and skin colors, the DNA of a single cell also contains the design of 206 bones, 600 muscles, a network of 10.000 auditory muscles, a network of 2 million optic nerves, and 100 billion nerve cells. (Google The Data Bank of Life: DNA) The cell uses this information quite flawlessly, in an exceedingly planned and coordinated manner, and in the appropriate places. Even before a human being has come into existence, his cells have already begun the process of building him. Because of these cells, we have the most advanced and sophisticated "plant" on earth to "build and construct" the human body, and it is all found and stored in DNA. The DNA is a self-replicating molecule that is carefully protected in the cell nucleus and functions as a kind of data bank for the human body. It is the carrier of specific genetic information that contains the complex instructions an organism needs to develop, live, and reproduce.

This information hidden inside the DNA controls and programs the thousands and thousands of different events that take place in the cells of the human body and in the functioning of its systems, as well as all physical features, from the color of a person's hair and eyes to his height, etc. Each cell not only functions individually, but also reproduces itself with all its vast DNA information and works in harmony with other cells. What is amazing is that within the DNA molecule found in a nucleus, which is far smaller than the microscopic cell where it is located, there exists a "data warehouse forty times bigger than the biggest encyclopedia of the world that includes millions of items of information for building the human body." (Google The Data Bank of Life: DNA)

Yet how can we ever talk of a molecule containing information? This is because what we talk about here is not a computer or library or a flash drive, but just an extremely tiny "piece of flesh" that is a hundred thousand times smaller than a millimeter and simply made up of protein, fat, and water molecules. It is truly a miracle of astounding proportions that this infinitesimal piece of flesh should contain and store even a single bit of information, let alone millions of bits. But what is the source of this wisdom? How is it that every single one of the 100 trillion cells in the human body possesses such unbelievable intelligence, information and ability? These cells are, after all, unconscious. You could never obtain a mind from it that will consciously organize any process and accomplish it.

How can it be then that DNA, which is composed of the arrangement of a certain number of unconscious atoms in certain sequences and enzymes, working in such a harmonious way, is able to organize countless complicated and diverse operations in the cell in a perfect and complete manner? The answer to this is quite simple. Wisdom is *not* in these molecules or in the cell that contains them, but in the one who has brought these molecules into being, programming them to function as they do. In short, wisdom is present not in the work done, but in the *creator* of that work. (See also "Proof: DNA Refutes Evolution" on YouTube.) Know that God created you and knows *everything* about you. The human body is truly God's masterpiece and designed with breathtaking complexity. All the basic chemicals in our body can be found here on earth. Yet these same chemicals cannot arrange themselves into cell tissues, organs and systems. This can only happen with the input of a divine creator having infinite wisdom and intelligence. The decision to still believe in evolution verses intelligent design, reflects a deep need to evade and totally block out the overwhelming evidence and logic that *proves* the universe was created by God.

In looking all around us, the order of the heavens, the galaxies, the planets, the detail and complexity of a DNA molecule, the function and sophistication of the human eye and brain, the beauty of music and color and sound, the miracle of birth, everywhere we turn we see God's magnificent work and creation. Yes, our loving God holds the planets in their orbits yet He knows *you* by name and the number of hairs on *your* head (Isaiah 43:1, Matt. 10:30). Why you ask? Because God tells us in the Bible that, "Long before He laid down earth's foundations, He had us in mind, had settled on us as the focus of His love, to be made whole and holy by His love. Long, long ago, He decided to adopt us into His family through Jesus Christ" (Eph.1:4 MSG). Oh how blessed we are! "God decided to give us life through the word of truth so we might be the *most important* of **all** the things He made" (James 1:18 NCV). What amazing love God has for us! His love not just for mankind in general, but His love for *you* in particular. God created you because He wants a relationship with you. He loves you. He wants you to know Him personally and intimately, and not just know about Him. Please, take the time therefore to learn more about God's loving message to you.

CHAPTER 4

How Did God Express and Convey His Deep Love for You?

"For God so loved the world, that He gave His only begotten Son, that whoever believes in Him should not perish, but have Eternal Life" (John 3:16 NASB). "I am your Father, and I love you even as I love My own son Jesus" (John 17:23 author paraphrase).

"Yet to all who did receive Him, to those who believe in His name, He gave the right to become children of God" (John 1:12 NIV). "See how great a love the Father has bestowed upon us, that we should be called children of God, and such we are" (1 John 3:1 NASB). "God decided to give us life through the word of truth, so we might be the _most important_ of **All** the things He made" (James 1:18 NCV). "And that neither death, nor life, nor angels, nor principalities, nor things present, nor things to come, nor powers, nor height, nor depth, nor any other created thing, shall be able to separate us from the love of God, which is in Christ Jesus our Lord" (Rom. 8:38-39 NASB).

Comment: God loves us enough to tell us the truth about how to be with Him and that there are only *two* destinations after life, and it will be necessary for us to choose the right path and destination while still alive, if we wish to be with Him in heaven. All roads do *not* lead to heaven. Only one does, and that is *through Jesus Christ.* Your salvation depends on what *Jesus* has done for you, not on what you do for Him. It is not our hold on our Lord that saves us. Rather it is the work of Jesus that justifies and saves us.

Jesus said, "I am the way . . . no one comes to the Father, but through Me" (John 14:6 NASB). Given the reality of two possible destinations, shouldn't we be eager and willing to pay *any price* to be with Him in heaven and to avoid hell? Yet, did you know the price has *already* been paid? "For you have been bought with a price" (1 Cor. 6:20 NASB). The amount paid was exorbitant, the shed blood of God's Son, Jesus Christ.

How did God express and convey His deep love for us? Consider this for a moment. Our Lord in His deep love for us determined He wants so much that we not go to hell, that *He* paid a *horrific* price on the cross so that we would not have to go. "For God did not send the Son into the world to judge the world, but that the world should be saved through Him" (John 3:17 NASB).

CHAPTER 5

If You Indeed Obey Him, What Does God Call You?

"Now therefore, if you will indeed obey My voice and keep My covenant, you shall be My treasured possession" (Ex. 19:5 ESV). "And we know that in all things God works for the good of those who love him, who have been called according to his purpose" (Rom. 8:28 NIV).

Yes, in all things God works for the good of those who love Him. However, we must realize that many people are not in God's family due to their unbelief, and as such, according to Scripture, they have no protection from the evil one, because "The angel of the Lord encamps all around those who fear Him, and rescues them" (Ps. 34:7 NASB).

Those who do not know the Lord and do not fear Him have no angels of protection! Scripture says, "The Lord is far from the wicked [and distances Himself from them]." However, if by chance they happen to be blessed with a Christian family member or friend who prays for them, then for a time they *will* have God's mercy extended to them. "But He hears the prayer of the [consistently] righteous, [that is, those with spiritual integrity and moral courage]" (Prov. 15:29 AMP).

Besides calling all *believers* "My Treasured Possession," God also describes us in another very special way. Scripture says, "To all who received him [Christ], to those who believed in His name, He gave the right to become children of God" (John 1:12 NIV).

"How blessed is God! And what a blessing He is! "Long before he laid down earth's foundations, he had us in mind, had settled on us as the focus of his love, to be made whole and holy by His love" (Eph. 1:4 MSG). "God decided to give us life through the Word of truth so we might be the most important of all the things He made" (James 1:18 NCV).

Because of all these things, can you think of anything more wonderful that could happen to you than receiving Christ? Do we cling and stick to our own understanding, that is, our own thoughts and beliefs about God, or do we accept the thought that God right now, may be seeking *our* attention, pleading we hear *His* message, and speaking to us through others, this book or the Bible? Please, dear friend, read on . . . hear Him.

CHAPTER 6

Does God Have Good Plans for You? Yes.

"For I know the plans I have for you, says the Lord. They are plans for good and not for disaster, to give you a future and a hope" (Jer. 29:11 NLT). "Let not your heart be troubled; believe in God, believe also in Me. In My Father's house are many dwelling places; if it were not so, I would have told you; for I go to prepare a place for you. And if I go and prepare a place for you, I will come again, and receive you to Myself; that where I am, *there* you may be also" (John 14:1-3 NASB). "The King [Jesus] will say . . . "Come, you who are blessed of My Father, inherit the Kingdom prepared for you from the foundation of the world" (Matt. 25:31, 34 NASB).

God who is the world architect and builder has prepared a magnificent place for us. It will be "prepared as a bride beautifully dressed for her husband" (Rev. 21:2 NIV). Our heavenly mansions are built, furnished, and waiting for occupancy and there's not a residence on this earth that can ever compare with what the Master Builder has carefully designed for His loving family. "Only those whose names are written in the Lamb's Book of Life will enter it" (Rev. 21:27 GW).

How does God describe this place He is preparing for us?

"The kingdom of heaven is like a [very precious] treasure hidden in the field, which a man found and hid again; then in his joy over it he goes and sells all he has and buys that field [securing the treasure for himself]" (Matt. 13:44 AMP).

"Again, the kingdom of heaven is like a merchant seeking fine pearls, and upon finding one pearl of great value, he went and sold all that he had, and bought it" (Matt. 13:45-46 NASB). You will not be in heaven two minutes before you cry out to yourself and say, "Why have I placed so much importance on things that were so temporary? What was I doing? Why have I wasted so much time, energy, and worry on things that were not going to last on earth?"

"Again, the kingdom of heaven is like a dragnet cast into the sea, and gathering fish of every kind; and when it was filled, they drew it up on the beach; and they sat down, and gathered the good fish into containers, but the bad they threw away. So it will be at the end of age; the angels will come forth, and take out the wicked from among the righteous, and will cast them into the furnace of fire; in that place there will be weeping and gnashing of teeth. Have you understood all these things?" (Matt. 13:47-51 NASB).

Many are deceiving themselves by believing they may have yet "another chance" after life. However, our Lord said, "Do not marvel at this; for an hour is coming in which all who are in the tombs shall hear His voice, and shall come forth, those who did the good deeds to a resurrection of life, those who committed the evil deeds to a resurrection of judgement" (John 5:28-29 NASB). "These will go away into eternal punishment, but the righteous into eternal life" (Matt. 25:46 NASB). There is no second chance after death. So who does the Lord have His eye on? "Behold, the eye of the Lord is on those who fear Him, on those who hope for His lovingkindness" (Ps. 33:18 NASB). "For the Eternal watches over the righteous, and His ears are attuned to their prayers. *He is always listening"* (Ps. 34:15 VOICE). He says, "I will instruct you and teach you in the way you should go; I will counsel you [who are willing to learn] with My eye upon you" (Ps. 32:8 AMP). Yes, by His very words, we know God has plans for good to all who listen and believe in Him.

CHAPTER 7

Has Jesus Been Misrepresented by Those Who Don't Know Him?

Yes, Scripture tells us He has been misrepresented by those who do not know Him. "Why do you not understand what I am saying? *It is* because you cannot hear My word. You are of *your* father the devil, and you want to do the desires of your father. He was a murder from the beginning, and does not stand in the truth, because there is no truth in him. Whenever he speaks a lie, he speaks from his own *nature*; for he is a liar, and the father of lies" (John 8:43-44 NASB).

"But because I speak the truth, you do not believe Me. Which one of you convicts Me of sin? If I speak truth, why do you not believe Me? He who is of God hears the words of God; for this reason you do not hear *them*, because you are not of God" (John 8:45-47 NASB).

Some of these people have missed the most important thing in life; they do not know God and thus have gone astray from the faith because of "worldly and empty chatter and the opposing arguments of what is falsely called 'knowledge' (see 1 Tim. 6:20-21 NASB). " . . . which the untaught and unstable distort, as they do also the rest of the Scriptures, to their own destruction. You therefore, beloved, knowing this beforehand, be on your guard so that you are not carried away by the error of unprincipled men and fall from your own steadfastness" (2 Peter 3:16-17 NASB). "He who overcomes shall not be hurt by the second death" (Rev. 2:11 NKJV).

Comment: Some compromise the gospel to avoid trouble or persecution. Do not be like that. The Lord counsels us to be strong in the faith. "This is My command: Be strong and courageous. Never be afraid or discouraged because I am your God, the Eternal One, and I will remain with you wherever you go" (Josh. 1:9 VOICE). Never be ashamed of the gospel of Christ. Never be ashamed to be identified with those who are being persecuted for their Christian faith. Throughout the world today there are many people who are enduring cruelties and persecution because of their faith. We must pray for them and for ourselves, so that in our own dying hour God will grant us mercy and grace to endure until the end, anticipating with certainty our reunion with Him.

Know that "Persecution comes because of the Word" (Matt. 13:21 NIV). Those who suffer for the sake of Christ will be blessed and should count it an honor to do so. Scripture says, "Blessed are those who have been persecuted for the sake of righteousness, for theirs is the kingdom of heaven. Blessed are you when people insult you and persecute you, and falsely say all kinds of evil against you because of Me. Rejoice and be glad, for your reward in heaven is great; for in the same way they persecuted the prophets who were before you" (Matt. 5:10-12 NASB).

As Scripture teaches, do not be carried away by the error of unprincipled men. But grow " . . . in the faith and knowledge of the Son of God, [growing spiritually] to become a mature believer, reaching to the measure of the fullness of Christ." Why? "So that we are no longer children [spiritually immature], tossed back and forth like ships in a stormy sea and carried about by every wind of doctrine, by the cunning and trickery of [unscrupulous] men, by the deceitful scheming of people ready to do anything for personal profit" (Eph. 4:13-14 AMP). Yes, as the Bible says, God has been misrepresented by those who do not know Him.

Part 2

Scriptural Summary Points to Remember

- I am your Creator. I know *everything* about you.

- You were in My care *before* you were born.

- You were predestined *before* I planned creation.

- Long before God laid down earth's foundations, He had us in mind, had settled on us as the focus of His love, to be made holy by His love.

- For all your days were written in My book *before* any one of them came to be.

- I am your Father, and I love you even as I love My own Son.

- For I have [eternal] plans for you says the Lord.

- If indeed we obey Him and keep His covenant, we shall be His *Treasured Possession.*

- God decided to give us life through the word of truth, so that we might be the *most important of all the things* He made.

- In My Father's house, I go and prepare a place for you.

- I have been misrepresented by those who do not know Me.

- Do not be carried away by the error of unprincipled men.

- I will instruct you and teach you in the way you should go; I will counsel you [who are willing to learn] with My loving eyes on you.

PART 3

God's Primary Message to Mankind:
"Listen to My Instruction"

CHAPTER 8

Exactly to Whom Should We Listen, with So Many Different Religions and Voices Worldwide?

"Listen, O my people, to My instruction; incline your ears to the words of My mouth" (Ps. 78:1 NASB). "Trust in the Lord with all your heart, and do not lean on your own understanding. In all your ways acknowledge him, and he will make your paths straight" (Prov. 3:5-6 ESV). "Do not trust in princes, (governments and leaders), in mortal man, in whom there is no salvation" (Ps. 146:3 NASB). "Fixing our eyes on Jesus, the author and perfecter of faith" (Heb. 12:2 NASB). "For I solemnly warned your fathers in the day that I brought them from the land of Egypt, even to this day, warning persistently, saying; Listen to My voice" (Jer. 11:7 NASB).

Comment: God's words of instruction are very clear for us. Just as all good loving parents want their young children to listen to them for wisdom and guidance, likewise, our heavenly Father for thousands of years has conveyed to His children over and over again to turn to Him, listen to Him, pay attention to Him, and to trust in Him for help and guidance and wisdom. Why? Because God dearly loves His children, He wants to protect us as we would do for our own children, and He does not want the errors of some people to mess with His children and lead them astray and down the wrong road called deception. When we lean on our own "limited" understanding or listen to the wrong voices, we are open to deception and our perspective becomes unbalanced, people around us may get hurt, and Satan is given a place instead. Thank God for those who can pull away the devil's cloak of deception. The blessings, peace, and wisdom are a result of listening and abiding in God's Word and learning that our heavenly Father is faithful to His Word.

Anytime you attend a religious service wherein the worship or teachings draws *away* from the Lord Jesus, or preaches something contrary to the gospel of Christ in the Bible, turn *away* from that religion! Don't be deceived! God clearly and explicitly tells us in Scripture, "Let your roots grow down into Him [Christ] and draw up nourishment from Him. See that you go on growing in the Lord, and become strong and vigorous in the truth" (Col. 2:7 TLB). "Remember what Christ taught, and let His words enrich your lives and make you wise" (Col. 3:16 TLB).

Don't let anybody come to you with teachings that distort or run contrary to Christ in the Bible. They cannot save you! Scripture tells us we are to be mature in stature, "till we all come to the unity of the faith and of the knowledge of the Son of God, to a perfect man, to the measure of the stature of the fullness of Christ" (Eph. 4:13 NKJV). The Bible is the source of knowledge and power and salvation. The Bible is the bedrock of truth and in it our Lord explicitly instructs for our own benefit to listen to Him, to His message. Get to know *His* Word.

CHAPTER 9

What Life-Saving Advice Does God Give His Children?

"Therefore, putting aside all malice and all deceit and hypocrisy and envy and all slander, like newborn babies, long for the pure milk of the word, [the Bible] so that by it you may grow in respect to salvation" (1 Peter 2:1-2 NASB). "This book of the law shall not depart from your mouth, but you shall meditate on it day and night, so that you may be careful to do according to all that is written in it" (Josh. 1:8 ESV). "My son, give attention to My words; Incline your ear to My sayings. Do not let them depart from your sight; Keep them in the midst of your heart. For they are LIFE to those who find them" (Prov. 4:20-22 NASB). "For I want you to understand what really matters" (Phil. 1:10 NLT). "Listen to the message of truth, the gospel of your salvation" (Eph. 1:13 author paraphrase).

"Listen *to this*! Behold, the sower went out to sow; as he was sowing, some seed fell beside the road, and the birds came and ate it up. Other seed fell on the rocky ground where it did not have much soil; and immediately it sprang up because it had no depth of soil. And after the sun had risen, it was scorched; and because it had no root, it withered away. Other seed fell among the thorns, and the thorns came up and choked it, and it yielded no crop. Other seeds fell into the good soil and as they grew up and increased, they yielded a crop and produced thirty, sixty, and a hundredfold." And Jesus said, "He who has ears to hear, let him hear. Do you not understand this parable?" (Mark 4:3-9,13 NASB). Jesus explains the parable . . .

"The sower sows the Word [of God]. These are the ones who are beside the road where the Word is sown; and when they hear, immediately Satan comes and takes away the Word which has been sown in them. And in a similar way these are the ones on whom seed was sown on the rocky places who, when they heard the Word, immediately receive it with joy; and they have no firm root in themselves, but are only temporary; then, when affliction or persecution arises because of the Word, immediately they fall away. And others are the ones on whom seed was sown among the thorns; these are the ones who have heard the word, and the worries of the world, and the deceitfulness of riches, and the desires for other things enter in and choke the Word, and it becomes unfruitful. And those are the ones on whom seed was sown on the good soil; and they hear the Word and accept it, and bear fruit, thirty, sixty, and a hundredfold" (Mark 4:14-20 NASB).

Jesus [not man] is our Lord, our teacher, our Savior, and our perfecter of faith. "And He was saying to them, 'Take care what you listen to'" (Mark 4:24 NASB). Therefore, listen to *His* message of truth, *to the gospel of Christ.* Knowing Christ and *His* message is the highest ambition in life. Jeremiah 9:23-24 ESV states, "Let not the wise man boast in his wisdom, let not the mighty man boast in his power, let not the rich man boast in his riches, but let him who boasts boast in this, that he *understands and knows Me.*" Remember, His message is life to those who find it.

CHAPTER 10

What Book Has God Instructed We Read?

"Seek from the book of the Lord, and read" (Isa. 34:16 NASB). "This book of the law shall not depart from your mouth, but you shall meditate on it day and night, so that you may be *careful* to do according to *all* that is written in it" (Josh. 1:8 NASB). "Every Word of God is flawless" (Prov. 30:5 NIV). "So get rid of all uncleanness and the rampant outgrowth of wickedness, and with a humble spirit, receive *and* welcome the Word, which implanted *and* rooted [in your hearts], contains the power to save your souls" (James 1:21 AMPC). "Listen, O my people, to my instruction; Incline your ears to the words of my mouth" (Ps. 78:1 NASB).

Comment: Paul, an apostle of Christ understood the power of prayer in gaining biblical understanding when he wrote, "I have not stopped… remembering you in prayers. I keep asking that the God of our Lord Jesus Christ …may give you a Spirit of wisdom and revelation, so that you may know Him better. I pray that the eyes of your heart may be enlightened" (Eph 1:16-18). Paul deeply sensed the importance and need for divine enlightenment through revelation from God, and he sought it through prayer. Likewise, no Christian believer should ever look down at the Word without first looking up at the very source of that Word and asking God in prayer for wisdom and guidance when reading from the book of the Lord.

Over and over in Scripture God instructs and commands that we are to seek from the book of the Lord and read. As Scripture says, "But grow in the grace and knowledge of our Lord and Savior Jesus Christ" (2 Peter 3:18 NASB). "Trust in the Lord with all your heart and do not lean on your own understanding" (Prov. 3:5 NASB). "Turn to My reproof" (Prov. 1:23 NASB). "My son, give attention to My wisdom. Incline your ear to My understanding" (Prov. 5:1 NASB). But why does God so emphasize that we listen to Him and trust His Word? Because God wants to protect us from possible deception, from the untaught and unstable who may distort the Scriptures. (See 2 Peter 3:16 NASB). "Therefore, [let me warn you] beloved, knowing these things beforehand, be on your guard so that you are not carried away by the error of unprincipled men [who distort doctrine] and fall from your steadfastness [of mind, knowledge, truth, and faith]" (2 Peter 3:17 AMP).

Some religions disagree with God's instructions and think otherwise. They say the Bible must be "interpreted" by the church! Therefore, the church becomes the "final authority," and its pronouncements are binding on its members. Learning of God's Word solely through the guidance of man and religion who "interprets" for Him is not only contrary to God's Word, but also allows for God's Word by accident or design to be tainted, to bring it more in line with the doctrines and beliefs of man and religion. Why not follow God's own *clear and repeated advice,* and listen to Him? Why not be allowed to think independently for yourself?

With what is happening worldwide with some of the religions today, it is evident that God has been grossly misrepresented by the clergy. If that statement is true, then that alone is conclusive proof that the clergy may not be representing God, especially if the Bible plainly proves that the doctrines they teach are wrong. Would it not be fair to let the Bible speak its claims for itself *before* you judge them? Judgment cannot be rendered with scholarly honesty unless the Scriptural evidence is first read!

So even if your basis of authority has been formed through your religion, or upbringing, or other source, why not see what the Bible has to say for itself? God used statements and language that He meant to be taken just as normally and plainly as the words in this book. So take it that way and believe He means what He says and let the *Bible* be the rule of law and reference standard. Remember, Scripture says in (Rom. 12:2 NLT): "Don't copy the behavior and customs of this world, but let GOD transform you into a new person by changing the way you think." He did not say let man or religion transform you, but let Him transform you. Trust Him. God said: "I don't want your sacrifices, I want your love; I don't want your offerings, I want you to know Me" (Hos. 6:6 TLB).

Know that the power to deceive is enormous when hundreds of millions of people have not read the Bible. Know also that to give greater credence to man and his religious doctrines over Christ and the Bible is to seriously err and violate God's direct instructions. Regardless of the teachings a church may preach, your allegiance should *always* be with your Creator, with God, and the Bible. Failure to follow our Lord's biblical instruction can seriously jeopardize one's security position. This is a decision that can cost you your eternal salvation! As the Bible has forewarned, why risk being carried away in doctrinal error and lose out on eternal salvation? I therefore ask, as God has instructed, that you carefully weigh the Scriptural evidence presented herein and read the book and judge for yourselves whether it is good to trust the plain teachings of the Bible and the sure guidance and magnificent promises of our Lord and Savior. Consider also, the following statements:

From Supreme Court Justices:

"The Bible is the best of all books, for it is the Word of God and teaches us the way to be happy in this world and in the next. Continue therefore to read it and to regulate your life by its precepts." -John Jay: First Chief Justice. "One of the beautiful boasts of our municipal jurisprudence is that Christianity is a part of the Common Law. ...There never has been a period in which the Common Law did not recognize Christianity as lying at its foundations. ...I verily believe Christianity necessary to the support of civil society." -Joseph Story: U.S. Supreme Court Justice.

From Supreme Court Rulings:

"Why may not the Bible, and especially the New Testament, without note or comment, be read and taught as a divine revelation in [schools] -its general precepts expounded, its evidences explained and its glorious principals of morality inculcated? ...Where can the purest principles of morality be learned so clearly or so perfectly as from the New Testament?" -Vidal v. Girard's Executors, 1844. In short summary the Bible has been historically recognized as the most important book for the development of both the rule of law and the democratic institutions in the Western world. No other religion, teaching, nation or movement has so changed the world for the better as Christianity has done. The Bible and the Ten Commandments have a moral and historical significance as well as religious meaning. They are the backbone and foundational requirements of a civil society and the jurist prudence of the American courts.

Example:

- Respect for life, as reflected in the commandment "Thou shalt not kill" and in homicide laws.
- Respect for property, as reflected in the commandment "Thou shalt not steal" and "Thou shalt not covet" and in property laws.

- Respect for family, as reflected in the commandment "Honor thy father and thy mother" and "Thou shalt not commit adultery" and in family laws.
- Respect for truth, as reflected in the commandment "Thou shalt not take the name of the Lord thy God in vain" and "Thou shalt not bear false witness" and in perjury and fraud laws.
- Respect for God, as reflected in the first four commandments and the recognition of God as the source of government authority and the source of human rights, etc.etc.

While Christianity today is under assault and the number of believers are dwindling, it might be appropriate to point out that Judeo-Christian tradition is what more than anything gave the West justice, liberty, the underlying morality of even many atheists, and the maintenance of a civil society. As Abraham Lincoln once said, the Bible is the best gift God has ever given to man. All the good from the Savior of the world is communicated to us through this book.

Know that the Bible prohibits anyone from revising the Holy Scriptures. Yet the urge to revise the Bible is as old as the Garden of Eden when the serpent came to Eve and asked, "Hath God said?" (see Gen. 3) Anybody who puts a question mark after the Word of God to discredit or distort its message is doing the work of the devil. God's Word is settled and sealed. Don't add to it. Don't dilute it. The Bible is clear. Don't fool with it. Proverbs 30:5-6 ESV declares, "Every Word of God proves true; He is a shield to those who take refuge in Him. Do not add to His words, lest He rebuke you, and you be found a liar." As God instructs over and over in the Bible, seek from the book of the Lord and read. "And in a humble spirit receive and welcome the Word which implanted and rooted [in your hearts] contains the power to save your souls" (James 1:21 ESV). Remember, "God decided to give us Life through the Word of Truth, so that we might be the *most important of all the things He made*" (James 1:18 NCV).

67

CHAPTER 11

Do We Err, Not Knowing the Scriptures? Yes, Absolutely.

"Jesus answered and said unto them, Ye do err, not knowing the scriptures, nor the power of God" (Matt. 22:29 KJV). "Some of these people have missed the most important thing in life - they don't know God" (1 Tim. 6:21 TLB). "Therefore, do not be unwise, but understand what the will of the Lord is" (Eph. 5:17 NKJV). "Seek from the book of the Lord, and read" (Isa. 34:16 NASB). "Make sure that the light you 'think' you have is not actually darkness" (Luke 11:35 NLT). "Trust in the Lord with all your heart, and do not lean on your own understanding" (Prov. 3:5 NASB).

Comment: As a nation, are we truly following God's instructions here? The answer is no! As a nation, we face a darkening time in our history when the forces of evil seem to be picking up momentum for an assault on the work of God in this world. The world's culture and governments are discrediting God, discrediting Christianity, and suppressing biblical truth. Like many, this nation is not going back to the culture and values it once held. *Roe v. Wade* may never be overturned. The sanctity of marriage is a relic of the past. God will never again be welcomed in our public schools. The Ten Commandments have already been removed from open display in our city schools and governmental buildings. States now allow minors to obtain abortion with no parental involvement required, and alternatively, states that do require parental permission may have a judge "excuse them" from this requirement!

The government's attempt to silence and control churches. The relentless effort to force Christian colleges and universities to abandon Christianity or face endless lawsuits and the possible cutting of funding. In America today, it is unconstitutional to use public schools to advance particular religious beliefs like Christianity. Specifically, public schools in America cannot promote Christianity nor sponsor both the study and practice of it. Furthermore, the Supreme Court ruled in *Abingdon v. Schempp* in 1963, that "no state law or public school board may require that passages from the Bible be read..." In that case they struck down "state action requiring that schools begin each day with readings from the Bible." They said: "morning devotional exercises in any form are constitutionally invalid."

Today our children are held, **by law**, to all our U.S. laws, deprived from the Bible, and denied the knowledge of the source of our own constitution and national jurisprudence controlling all of our society's laws. Yet John Adams, one of the Founding Fathers who served as Vice president and President of the United States said this: "...the Bible is the best book in the world." Why is the Bible, the book that gave birth to education for the masses in the first place, to be so banned as described above in all our public schools?

As Christians, we are living in a hostile environment that constantly seeks to pull us and our children *away* from God. Yet, if we truly think we can solve our problems in the world without God and His commandments, then we are living in a fool's paradise.

Know this: The devil's top overriding goal is to block God's work, and if he can convince you God doesn't really care or love you, or that you cannot fully trust Him and do not really need Him, then he has succeeded in blocking God's work in *your life* and achieved his goal. Recognize that Satan, through your mind, will contest every single minute you spend in Bible study, prayer, and reading this book! As our Creator clearly indicated, we do err, not knowing the Scriptures or the power of God.

CHAPTER 12

How Do We Acquire Saving Faith; How Does Faith Come?

"So then faith *comes* by hearing, and hearing by the Word of God" (Rom. 10:17 NKJV). "Listen, O my people, to My instruction, Incline your ears to the words of My mouth" (Ps. 78:1 NASB). "All scripture is inspired by God and is useful to teach us what is true, and to make us realize what is wrong in our lives. It corrects us when we are wrong and teaches us to do what is right" (2 Tim. 3:16 NLT).

Comment: There are two kinds of listeners: passive and aggressive. A passive listener does not come to God to hear a decision from Him. The aggressive listener comes knowing and seeking to hear diligently what God has to say. We are not simply to hear but also to obey, not simply to glance at the Word of God but also to grasp the Word. We are either in the process of resisting God's truth or in the process of welcoming it and being *shaped and molded* by it.

No one can believe God and the Bible unless God enables him to believe. And how does God enable you to believe? He gives you the Word. Faith "comes" by *reading and meditating and abiding* upon the Word in the Bible and thrives in an atmosphere of prayer. The verse above says that faith "comes." You do not generate it. It "comes." God gives it. Let your Bible begin to saturate your mind and soul every day. Listen to God's words in Scripture, and then you will "believe it and receive it."

Faith is not an achievement we can earn for ourselves, even if we study the Bible for forty years. It is an endowment that is given to us by God. Believing and understanding God's Word the way *He* (not religion) wants you to understand is something that is granted to us, given to us, by God. Scripture says faith without works is dead. In other words, true faith *must* do more than merely believe; it also obeys!

Jesus said, "If anyone loves Me, he will keep (obey) My Word" (John 14:23 NASB). If what you say you believe does not translate itself into *action*, then you really do not believe it. Know that our heavenly Father dearly loves you and is pleading that you become His child through faith in Christ Jesus. "That Christ may dwell in your hearts through faith; that you, being rooted and grounded in love, may be able to comprehend with all the saints what is the width and length and depth and height— to know the love of Christ which passes knowledge; that you may be filled with all the fullness of God" (Eph. 3:17-19 NKJV). Read about some of the great heroes of faith in Hebrews 11 of your Bible.

So how then does Scripture say we are to acquire Saving Faith? Answer; Like new born babies, long for the pure milk of the word, so that we may grow in respect to salvation. Because faith comes from hearing the Word of God. By listening to His instruction, by inclining our ears to the words of *His* mouth and as Scripture declares, "That our faith should *not* rest on the wisdom of men, but on the Power of God" (1 Corinthians 2:5 NASB). In a summary statement we are to seek, welcome and grasp hold of *God's* word, and being shaped molded and living by it.

CHAPTER 13

Friendship with God Is Reserved for Whom, and What Did God Promise those Friends?

" Friendship with God is reserved for those who reverence him, [who love, honor, respect, believe, trust, and obey him]. With them alone, He shares the secrets of His promises" (Ps. 25:14 TLB). "This is the promise which He Himself made to us: eternal life" (1 John 2:25 NASB). "And this is the way to have eternal life, by knowing you, the only true God, and Jesus Christ, the one you sent to earth!" (John 17:3 TLB). "And the testimony is this, that God has given us eternal life, and this life is in His Son" (1 John 5:11 NASB).

Jesus declared and reaffirmed: "Truly, truly, I say to you, whoever hears My word and believes Him who sent Me, has eternal life, and does not come into judgment, but has passed from death to life" (John 5:24 ESV). "But the scripture says that the whole world is under the power of sin; and so the gift which is promised on the basis of faith in Jesus Christ is given to those who *believe*" (Gal. 3:22 GNT).

Comment: Remember, God's friendship and promises are reserved and open to all who reverence and believe in Him. God will never force His will on you. You are free to choose. But you are not free to choose the consequences of your choice. Jesus went to such great lengths in teaching that there is an eternal destiny for each person, either eternal life (heaven) or eternal damnation (hell).

The eternal destiny of each individual depends on a decision made in this life (see Luke 16:19-31). Unfortunately, we are so caught up with the affairs of this life that we give no attention to eternity. Yet what you decide to do with God's Word in this life decides where you shall spend eternity in the next. And eternity is but a breath away!

Remember, Satan bombards our minds with so many things that there is no room for God anymore. It becomes difficult for God to speak to our hearts when our minds are so cluttered with other things. Satan will do all he can to detour our minds away from the important task at hand, and that is *listening to what God has to say*. Yieldedness is so *vital* in listening to what He has to say to us. If we grieve God by saying yes to sin and quench the Spirit by saying no to God, then the message of God cannot be delivered because we are not listening. To listen openly means to be willing to hear God correct us as well as comfort us, to hear God convict us as well as assure us.

CHAPTER 14

Exactly How Did God Say We Can Gain More Understanding of His Will?

"Pay close attention to what you hear. The closer you listen, the more understanding you will be given—and you will receive even more" (Mark 4:24 NLT). "To those who listen to My teaching, [not men's and different religious teachings] more understanding will be given. But for those who are not listening, even what little understanding they have will be taken away from them" (Mark 4:25 NLT).

Comment: The Bible instructs us, "And do not be conformed to this world, but be transformed by the renewing of your mind, that you may prove what the will of God is, that which is good and acceptable and perfect" (Rom. 12:2 NASB). Yes, God wants us to know His will. It is one of the greatest gifts to mankind, given to lead man into a full, abundant life, to protect him from deception and lead him into eternal life. All the evil extent in the world today is caused by disobedience of our Creator's laws. Throughout Scripture, God is saying over and over again, *listen to Me. Pay attention to Me. Follow Me.*

God has important things in the Bible to tell you and wants to share this with you, but it's incumbent upon you to listen, to pay attention. You must earnestly be willing to know God's will and He will help you.

Understand that not only is God's guidance promised, but guidance is also *provisional!* You must be willing to listen, to listen to His teachings, and the closer you listen, the more understanding you will be given. You will acquire understanding to the degree you spend listening to God's Word. Each promise in Scripture is a written agreement from God, which you may plead before Him with this reasonable request: Please, Lord, do as thou hast said, and give me understanding, and "Strengthen me according to Your Word" (Ps. 119:28 NASB).

God will answer you but remember, you have to *yield* to the will of God. It's not enough to hear God. It is not enough to just know the will of God. You have to say, "I am ready to *do your will!*" If you are not willing to yield to the will of God, why should God show you more of His will? God speaks to those who are sincere and wanting to listen and learn and abide in God's will. And to know and abide in God's will is the highest of all wisdom. Our faith and obedience to God's will is the key, and it unlocks God's power to help us. It is all dependent upon your faith, or lack of it.

As the Bible declares, "According to your faith, be it done to you" (Matt. 9:29 ESV). Christian biblical faith is the greatest asset we have. It is the means of exchange into God's heavenly kingdom. Unbelief is the opposite. Unbelief is the highest ranking and *gravest* sin. Unbelief caused Adam and Eve to sin against God. The Bible says: "Whoever believes in Him is not condemned, but whoever does not believe is condemned already, because he has not believed" (John 3:18 ESV). It is unbelief that shuts the door to God's kingdom.

Through the Bible and other means, God speaks but not everyone will listen or believe. Out of love and divine patience God *pleads* with people but some refuse to listen, to believe. They question, they doubt, they debate. They parade God's Word they hear past the judgment bar of their own mind and say, "No, I don't think I'll believe that." But God says unbelief does not come out of the mind but out of the heart. He says, "Beware . . . lest there be in any of you an evil heart of *unbelief* in departing from the living God" (Heb. 3:12 NKJV).

Don't become so conformed to this world and so well adjusted to its culture that you fit into it without even thinking of God. Instead, fix your attention on God. You'll be changed from the inside out . . . unlike the culture around you, always dragging you down to its level of immaturity. God brings the best out of you, developing well-formed maturity in you. As Scripture says; "And the Lord who is the Spirit makes us more and more like Him as we are changed into His glorious image" (2 Cor. 3:18 NLT).

Get to know God. No one who consistently breaks God's laws can have real peace of mind. He will have fears and frustrations and often a guilty conscience. But the person who keeps God's laws has a clear conscience. He is at peace with God, with himself, and with his neighbor. He has the "peace of God, which surpasses all understanding" (Phil. 4:7 NKJV).

So how do you gain more understanding of His will? Scripture tells us to pay close attention to what you hear. The closer you listen to *His* teachings, the more understanding you will be given. Yield to the will of God and according to your faith it *will* be done to you.

CHAPTER 15

Why Did Jesus Speak to Great Multitudes in Parables, and What Important Life-saving Message Can We Learn and Apply from This?

Then the disciples came to Him and asked, "Why do You speak to the crowds in parables?" Jesus replied to them, "To you it has been granted to know the mysteries of the kingdom of heaven, but to them it has not been granted." [Why?] "For whoever has [spiritual wisdom because he is *receptive* to God's word], to him *more* will be given, and he will be richly *and* abundantly supplied; but whoever does not have [spiritual wisdom because he has devalued God's Word], even what he has will be taken away from him. This is the reason I speak to the crowds in parables: because while [having the power of] seeing they do not see, and while [having the power of] hearing they do not hear, nor do they understand *and* grasp [spiritual things]" (Matt. 13:10-13 AMP).

In them the prophecy of Isaiah is being fulfilled, which says; "You will hear and keep on hearing, but never understand; and you will look and keep on looking, but never comprehend; For this nation's heart has grown hard, and with their ears they hardly hear, and they have [tightly] closed their eyes, otherwise they would see with their eyes, and hear with their ears, and understand with their heart, and turn [to Me] and I would heal them [spiritually]" (Matt. 13:10-15 AMP).

Comment: Do you understand the meaning of Jesus' message here? To believers who are *genuinely receptive* and listen to His Word, God will *extend and grant* to them wisdom and understanding to reveal His Kingdom truth, but to unbelievers and those who devalue and discredit our Lord, the truth shall be *concealed* from them. Those to whom God has sovereignly given eternal life through Christ are the true citizens of His Kingdom. Of such persons Jesus says; "*to him more shall be given.*"

Believers receive additional light of truth as they grow in obedience and belief and maturity in the Lord. As believers remain faithful, God reveals more and more light until they "have an abundance." In contrast, divine truth is *concealed* from false citizens of the Kingdom because of their unbelief in the gospel of Christ and lack of obedience. Understand that it is having Christ that counts. The human race is called on throughout the Bible to repent of our sins and to believe in Christ.

Thousands heard Jesus' teachings including the parables, and saw His miracles, but most did not recognize Him as the Messiah, nor receive Him as their Lord and Savior.

Because such unbelievers refuse God's light as it shines on them, He conceals it from them and they drift further into spiritual darkness. All people are either progressing or regressing spiritually. The longer that believers trust and abide in Christ, the *more* He reveals His truth and power to them. And the longer unbelievers deny and reject His words and authority and what little knowledge they may have of the gospel of Christ, the less of God's truth they will understand. It is therefore vitally important to be on the right side of the revealing-concealing equation. Jesus said; "Learn from *Me*" (Matt. 11:29 NASB). Remember what **Christ** taught, and let *His* words enrich your lives and make you wise" (Colossians 3:16 TLB).

The Bible can never be properly understood as God wants it understood, unless God reveals it to you. One cannot come to an understanding of God's will apart from the Holy Spirit's *illumination* and your *adherence* to Christ's Word. We are commanded, "Only conduct yourselves in a manner worthy of the gospel of Christ; . . . standing firm in one spirit, with one mind striving together for the faith of the gospel" (Phil. 1:27 NASB). "Let the Word of Christ richly dwell within you" (Col. 3:16 NASB).

Do you understand why these words were said? All these Biblical instructions and the *adherence* to them are so vitally important in gaining understanding. Does the Word of Christ richly dwell within *you*? Are you a true believer of Jesus Christ? Have you bowed your knee to Him? Is He Lord over your life? If so, the Holy Spirit who resides within you will give you illumination and a rightful understanding of this book. If you are not a child of God because you don't believe nor abide in Christ's Word, then you do not have the Holy Spirit to give you this illumination and understanding. You may study them for 50 years but you will never have the wisdom nor understanding as God *would want you to have*. The Bible is a closed book to those who reject our Lord and Savior Jesus Christ.

As Jesus said, "I am the Light of the world; he who follows Me, will not walk in the darkness, but will have the light of Life" (John 8:12 NASB). Don't refuse His light as it shines on you! "Believe in the light while you have the light, so that you may become children of the light" (John 12:36 NIV). Jesus said, "If you continue in My word, *then* you are truly disciples of Mine; and you will know the truth, and the truth will make you free" (John 8:31-32, NASB). "I am the way, and the truth, and the life; no one comes to the Father but through Me" (John 14:6 NASB).

"He has told you, O man, what is good, and what the Lord really wants from you. He wants you to promote justice, to be faithful, and to live obediently before your God" (Micah 6:8 NET). "Give unto the Lord the glory due to His name" (Psalm 29:2 NKJV). "Don't despise what God has revealed" (1 Thess. 5:20 GW). "Do not quench [subdue, or be unresponsive to the working and guidance of] the Holy Spirit"

(1 Thess. 5:19 AMP). Why? Because Scripture says "The person without God's Spirit doesn't accept the things that come from the Spirit of God. These things are foolish to them. They can't understand them. In fact, such things *can't* be understood without the Spirit's help" (1 Corin. 2:14 NIV). So welcome His Word. Don't quench the Spirit and don't despise His Word. Know that God dearly loves us and that He is so ever ready to help and guide and illuminate His will and understanding to us. Remember however, it is incumbent that we first be genuinely receptive *and* listen to His Word. Obedience is key.

CHAPTER 16

To Those Who Are Serious about Finding God, Will God Make Sure You Won't Be Disappointed? Yes.

"My son, if you will receive My words and treasure My commandments within you, make your ear attentive to wisdom, incline your heart to understanding; for if you cry for discernment, lift your voice for understanding; If you seek for her as silver and search for her as hidden treasures; *then*, you will discern the fear of the Lord, and discover the knowledge of God" (Prov. 2:1-5 NASB).

"When you come looking for Me, you'll find Me. Yes, when you get serious about finding Me, and want it more than anything else, I'll make sure you won't be disappointed. God's Decree" (Jer. 29:13 MSG).

Comment: With the word *if* used three times in the first paragraph above, Jesus made a conditional promise that you may know the truth and the truth can set you free. However, this means your spiritual growth is directly proportionate to the amount of time and effort you put into the study of His Word, and that you gain access to His truths by believing in Him and holding and abiding to His teaching. Remember, if you're not willing to believe and yield to the will of God, why should God show you His will?

No spiritual wisdom is more important than the reading of God's Holy Word. Nothing can substitute for it. There is simply no healthy Christian life that can be learned apart from the diet of the milk and meat of Holy Scripture. The reasons for this are obvious. In the Bible God tells us about Himself and especially about Jesus Christ, the Incarnation of God. The Bible discloses the mind of God, reveals the state of man, points out the way to salvation, the doom of sinners, and the magnificent promises to those who believe in the Lord. Its doctrines are holy, its precepts are binding, its histories are true, and its judgements are unchangeable. Read it to be wise, believe it to be safe, and practice it to be holy. It contains light to direct you.

It also reveals how Jesus suffered and died for us as a sinless, willing substitute for breaking God's laws, and how we must repent and believe in Him to be right with God. None of this eternally essential information can be found anywhere else except in God's book called the Holy Bible. Scripture says, ". . . making the very most of your time [on earth, recognizing and taking advantage of each opportunity and using it with wisdom and diligence], because the days are [filled with] evil. Therefore do not be foolish *and* thoughtless, but understand *and* firmly grasp what the will of the Lord is" (Eph. 5:16-17 AMP).

CHAPTER 17

What Specific Instruction Has God Given about the "World's Standards," and to Whom Exactly Does God Share the Secrets of His Covenant?

"And do not be conformed to this world, but be transformed by the renewing of your mind, [as you mature spiritually] so that you may prove what the will of God is, that which is good and acceptable and perfect" (Rom. 12:2 NASB). "Listen, O My people, to My instruction; Incline your ears to the words of My mouth" (Ps. 78:1 NASB). "Anyone willing to be corrected is on the pathway to life. Anyone refusing has lost his chance" (Prov. 10:17 TLB).

"Therefore do not be foolish, but understand what the will of the Lord is" (Eph. 5:17 ESV). "Do not reject the discipline of the Lord or loathe His reproof" (Prov. 3:11 NASB). "My people are destroyed for lack of knowledge, because you have rejected knowledge" (Hos. 4:6 NASB). "So the people without understanding are ruined" (Hos. 4:14 NASB).

Comment: God shares the secrets of His covenant to those who *listen to Him*, to those who do not reject the discipline of the Lord. It is important to understand and live by the will of the Lord. Before we accept anything in our lives, we need to filter it through God's Word and eliminate anything that opposes His will or grieves His Spirit. If the condition or the act is contrary to God's Word, it should be purged. Do not be conformed to the standards of the world.

This is why we must learn to listen to Him because God's Word reveals the innermost intentions and motivations of our lives and what is going on about us. When we believe the Word of God, it uncovers the veil so that we "see" the reality of all that is about us. The light of the Word illuminates everything, enabling us to discern right from wrong and truth from error. Whatever we see or hear or read, we must thoroughly check it out against the absolute standard of God's truth. "Therefore, be ye not unwise, but understand what the will of the Lord is" (Eph. 5:17 KJ21). "Listen O My people to My instructions" (Ps. 78:1 NASB). "Everyone on the side of truth listens to Me" (John 18:37 NIV). "Anyone who listens to My teaching and follows it is wise" (Matt. 7:24 NLT). "Anyone who hears My teachings and doesn't obey it is foolish" (Matt. 7:26 NLT). "Trust in God, and trust also in Me" (John 14:1 NLT).

A backyard of brown and burnt grass that gets just a trickle of water or no water at all cannot be expected to grow and flourish in a thick and rich green color. It needs lots of water! Likewise, not being receptive and getting no reading of Scripture or just a trickle of God's Word here and there will not cut it either. Just as we would fully open the water hose to "flood and drench" the lawn starving of water, we need to do likewise and "flood and drench" our mind and soul with vast amounts of God-given life-sustaining spiritual wisdom and understanding of His Word, and that only from God's approved book, the Holy Bible. And for sustaining flourishing spiritual growth, God wants us to shower our minds *daily* with His Word (see Josh. 1:8).

As we close Part 3 of this book, understand that the primary message God conveyed to all mankind with persistent warning is to understand His will, listen to His Word, His instruction, and like newborn babies, long for the pure milk of the Word. He says "Receive and welcome" the Word which, implanted and rooted in our hearts, contains the power to save our souls. For they are *life* to those who believe. "Stop doubting and believe" (John 20:27 NIV). The Bible affirms, "Have faith in God" (Mark 11:22 NKJV).

Part 3

Scriptural Summary Points to Remember

- Listen, O My people to My instruction, give attention to My words for they are life to those who find them.

- Do not lean on your own understanding, but seek from the book of the Lord and read.

- Meditate on it day and night so not to be carried away by error and false religions.

- Fix your eyes on Jesus, the author and perfecter of faith.

- Receive and welcome *His Word*, which has the power to save your soul.

- Remember what Christ taught, and let His words enrich your lives and make you wise.

- The closer you listen, the *more* understanding you will be given.

- Remember, faith comes by hearing, and hearing by the word of our Lord.

- Do not be conformed to the world. They err not knowing Scripture.

- Trust in the Lord with all your heart.

- Understand and *firmly grasp* what the will of the Lord is.

- God's Word, the Bible, can never be properly understood apart from the Holy Spirit's illumination. This illumination is *conditional* on believing and abiding in Christ's Word. Therefore, one must believe and abide in Christ's Word to *gain* Scriptural wisdom and understanding.

- Remember: Scripture says that the whole world is under the power of sin; and so the gift which is promised on the basis of faith in Jesus Christ is *given to those who believe.*

PART 4

Jesus Christ, His Absolute Authority, and the Only Source of Salvation

CHAPTER 18

For What Reason Was Jesus Christ Born?

Jesus said, "In fact, the reason I was born and came into the world is to testify to the truth. Everyone on the side of truth, listens to Me" (John 18:37 NIV). "For I do not speak on my own initiative, but the Father himself who sent Me, has given Me a commandment as what to say and what to speak." I know that His commandment is eternal life; therefore the things I speak, I speak just as the Father has told Me" (see John 12:49-50 NASB; John 17:8 ESV; John 3:34 NASB). "Therefore do not be ashamed of the testimony of our Lord" (2 Tim. 1:8 NASB). "I assure you, most solemnly I tell you, he who believes in Me, [who adheres to, trusts in, relies on, and has faith in Me], has eternal life" (John 6:47 AMPC). "And this is eternal life, that they know you, the only true God, and Jesus Christ whom you have sent" (John 17:3 ESV).

"And the testimony is this, that God has given us eternal life, and this life is in His Son. He who has the Son has life; He who does not have the Son of God does not have life" (1 John 5:11-12 NASB). "Whoever denies the Son, does not have the Father" (1 John 2:23 NASB). " . . . because he has not believed in the testimony that God has given concerning His Son"

(1 John 5:10 NASB). "Truly, truly, I say to you, whoever hears My word and believes Him who sent Me has eternal life. He does not come into judgment, but has passed from death to life" (John 5:24 ESV). "For this reason also [because He obeyed and so completely humbled Himself], God has highly exalted Him, and bestowed on Him the name which is above every name, so that at the name of Jesus, every knee shall bow [in submission], of those who are in heaven and on earth and under the earth" (Phil. 2:9-10 AMP). "And let all the angels of God worship Him" (Hebrews 1:6 KJV).

Comment: Our Heavenly Father dearly loves us and wants to protect us from sin, deception and the demonic influence from Satan. God see's the multiple thousands of different and false religions and denominations worldwide, each claiming to not only represent God, but to also having the exclusive knowledge and "true way" to eternal salvation. God see's many of the churches have been led for centuries by apostates who changed the grace of God into a license for immorality, and to deny the words and authority of Jesus Christ our Lord and savior. He see's these religious leaders making themselves into the arbiters of salvation, the "holy priests," and diminished Christ's sacrifice through traditions that demand "certain works" in exchange for the forgiveness of sins and the entry into Heaven. He see's some church leaders claiming to be infallible and that one need not believe in Jesus Christ to be saved!! For these and other reasons, God sent His Son to set the record straight, to bear witness and testify to the truth. His authority stands far and above that of any religious denomination. Truly, what greater authority or better source can we possibly have than the Son of God for truth and guidance?

Jesus' teachings are *superior* to anyone else's in the world because His knowledge is not secondhand. He is the *source* of divine revelation from the Father. Consider this: What greater weight or more authoritative person can anyone ever have on the face of this earth, than the Son of God to bear witness and to testify to the truth! Jesus said He does not speak on His own initiative, but in obedience to the Father Himself who sent Him. Christ *is* the truth. The very conveyance of His words, His actions, His life, and His death on earth, and the gospel He left us demonstrate just how deeply caring and how great His love is for us. The evidence is overwhelming! Who would ever do for us all that He did for us?

The whole purpose behind Christ's coming was to die for us and pay the penalty for sin. In doing so He bore witness and testified to the truth about God's message, that He loves us, that we are to receive and welcome His Word, and treasure His commandments, and that sin kills, hell is real, God is merciful, Christ can save us, and that Christ is our *only* Savior. Your faith should therefore *never* rest solely on the wisdom of man and his beliefs. It is what Christ Jesus says that counts! And every Christian is predestined and called to become Christlike. "For those whom He foreknew He also predestined to be the image of His Son" (Rom. 8:29, ESV).

In whom exactly does the God of the Bible ask you to believe? It is not man and it is not religion. Neither can save you! The God of the Bible says, "Believe in the Lord Jesus, and you shall be saved" (Acts 16:31 NASB) and "Let the Word of Christ richly dwell within you" (Col. 3:16 NASB). Jesus said, "If anyone loves Me, he will keep My Word; and My Father will love him, and we will make our abode with him" (John 14:23 NASB).

Question: When do you believe you get eternal life? When you die and go to heaven? The answer is no! If you do not have eternal life before you die, you will not get it thereafter when they bury or cremate you. You get eternal life the moment you *believe* and *abide* in Jesus Christ. Jesus said, "It's urgent that you listen carefully to this: Anyone here who believes what I am saying right now and aligns himself with the Father, who has in fact put Me in charge, has at this very moment the real, lasting Life and is no longer condemned to be an outsider. This person has taken a giant step from the world of the dead to the world of the living" (John 5:24 MSG).

Notice that Jesus said, "*is no longer condemned.*" Jesus came to give us present tense everlasting life. Do you have eternal life right now? If you sincerely believe and abide in Jesus Christ, you have it right now! When do you get it? When you believe! Again, as Scripture confirms in (Acts 16:31 KJV): "Believe on the Lord Jesus Christ, and thou shalt be saved."

CHAPTER 19

Exactly Who Is Jesus Christ?

" **A**braham, Isaac, and Jacob are their ancestors, and Christ himself was an Israelite as far as his human nature is concerned. And He *is* God, the one who rules over everything and is worthy of eternal praise! Amen" (Rom 9:5 NLT). There are numerous other scriptures throughout the Bible that give evidence for the absolute deity of Jesus Christ. The following is but a short list of such evidence confirming His divine nature.

1. **Who is Jesus Christ?**

    A comparison of both the Old and New Testament provides a powerful testimony as to Jesus Christ's identity as God. For example, a study of the Old Testament states that it is *only* God who saves. In Isaiah 43:11 (NKJV), God declares and asserts: "I, even I, am the Lord, and beside Me there is no savior." This verse clearly points out that there is only one Savior, the Lord God, and there is no other. It is therefore highly revealing of Christ's divine nature that the New Testament clearly refers to *Him* as "our great God and Savior Christ Jesus" (Titus 2:13 NKJV).

2. **Who is the Creator of all things?**

   Likewise, in comparing the Old and New Testaments, God declared in Isaiah 44:24 (NASB): "I, the Lord, am the maker of all things, stretching out the heavens by Myself and spreading out the earth all alone." The fact that God Himself declared that He alone is "the maker of all things," and the accompanying fact that Jesus Christ is claimed to be the Creator of "all things" in John 1:3 and Heb 1:2, proves that Christ is truly God. There can be no misunderstanding of Christ's divine nature when Scripture states that "for by Him [Christ], all things were created that are in heaven and that are on earth, visible and invisible, whether thrones or dominions or principalities, or powers. All things were created through Him and for Him" (Col 1:16 NKJV). "Know that the Lord Himself is God; It is He who made us" (Psalm 100:3 NASB).

3. **Who does the Bible accord all divine honor, reverence, and worship?**

   The Bible accords all divine honor to Jesus (see John 5:23 NASB), prayer (John 14:14 NASB), and reverence (Eph 5:21 NASB). It credits Him with doing God's works, such as creating and sustaining the world (John 1:1–3,14 NASB; Col 1:16–17 KJV; Heb 1:2–3, 10 NASB). Jesus was also worshiped on many occasions. He accepted worship from Thomas (John 20:28), from the angels (Heb 1:6), the wise men (Matt 2:11), the blind beggar (John 9:38), Mary Magdalene (Matt 28:9), and His disciples (Matt 28:17).

   Scripture further states that "at the name of Jesus, every knee shall bow [in submission], of those who are in heaven and on earth and under the earth, and that every tongue will confess *and* openly acknowledge that Jesus Christ is Lord (sovereign God)" (Phil 2:10-11 AMP). "Oh come, let us worship and bow down; Let us kneel before the Lord our Maker. For He *is* our God" (Psalms 95:6-7 NKJV). "As surely as I live, says the Lord, Everyone will bow before Me; *everyone* will say that I **am** God" (Rom. 14:11 NCV). It should be noted that Scripture is very clear: *Only* God can be worshiped (see Deut 6:13; Exodus 34:14; Matt 4:10). In view of this command that only God can be worshiped and the fact that *both* humans and angels and those in heaven worshiped Jesus, we can see that Scripture clearly demonstrates that Jesus is God.

4. **Who claimed to be God and have the power of God?**
    Not only did Jesus claim to be God, but He also claimed to have the power of God. By His very own statements and actions, He gave evidence that He has the power to judge the nations (Matt 25:31–46), to raise people from the dead (John 5:25–29), and to forgive sins (Mark 2:5–7), something that only God can do (Isa 43:25). But Jesus' identity isn't based only on what He says, but also on what He does and He left irrefutable evidence in the divine record that He is God.

5. **Does the Bible also confirm that Jesus is God in the flesh?**
    Yes! "In the beginning was the Word, and the Word was with God, and the Word was God" (John 1:1 NASB); "and the Word became flesh, [Jesus] and dwelt among us..." (John 1:14 NASB); "...and from whom, according to the flesh, Christ *came*, who is over all, *the* eternally blessed God" (Romans 9:5 NKJV). Jesus is God incarnate, God in human form, the express image of the Father, who, without ceasing to be God, became man in order that He might demonstrate who God is, and to provide the means of salvation for humanity (Matt 1:21; Colossians 1:14).

6. **Who purchased the church of God with His own blood?**

   Acts 20:28 (NKJV) tells us "to shepherd the church of God which He [God] purchased with His own blood." And who purchased the Church with His own blood? Jesus Christ (see Eph 1:5, 7). This same verse in Acts declares that God purchased His Church with His own blood. Therefore, Jesus is God in the flesh.

7. **How did Jesus respond when Philip asked Him to show him God the Father?**

   In John 14:8 (NKJV), Philip asked Jesus, "Lord, show us the Father and it is sufficient for us." How did Jesus respond to Philip's request? Jesus said to him, "Have I been with you so long, and yet you have not known Me, Philip? He who has seen Me has *seen* the Father; so how can you say, 'Show us the Father'? Do you not believe that I am in the Father, and the Father in Me? Believe Me that I am in the Father and the Father in Me" (John 14:9–11 NKJV).

8. **Who does Jesus say He is?**

   And Jesus said to them, "You are from below, I am from above; you are of this world, I am not of this world. Therefore I said to you that you will die in your sins; for unless you believe that I am *He* [the Father], you will die in your sins" (John 8:23–24, 27 NASB).

9. **Cults and False Religions:**

   Today there are many cults and false religions that deny God's divine Word, the Bible, and all that Jesus claimed to be. Sometimes it's for lack of understanding. We must bear in mind, however, that it is impossible for us to always fully understand how God works. But not understanding is not a reason for not believing in Him. We as human beings with such limited minds cannot expect to have the capacity to fully comprehend and grasp all the doings of our awesome and infinite God. As Scripture tells us, "Human wisdom is so tiny, so impotent, next to the seeming absurdity of God. Human strength can't begin to [even] compete with God's weakness" (1 Cor 1:24 MSG). But we are not asked to comprehend all of God's actions. We are asked to know *Christ* and with real certainty (see Col 2:2 TLB). False religions and cults will often disagree with the Bible and raise objections against the deity of Christ. In what follows in Numbers 10 through 14, their key objections will be briefly summarized and answered.

10. Jesus is praying to the Father.

Some religious cults and people believe that because Jesus prayed to the Father, He could not also be God. Biblically, however, it was in His humanity that Jesus prayed to the Father. Positionally speaking, as a man and a teacher, "in all things He had to be made like His brethren" (Heb 2:17). Because Jesus came as a man, and because one of His duties as a man was to set an example and to worship and pray to God, it was perfectly normal for Jesus to address the Father in prayer, but this should not in any way detract from His deity.

11. Jesus is not all-knowing.

Some religious cults argue that because Jesus stated that no one knew the day or the hour of His return except the Father (Mark 13:32), Jesus must not then be all-knowing, and therefore He must not be God. In response, Jesus, in the Gospels, sometimes spoke from the perspective of His divinity, and at other occasions from the perspective of His humanity. In Mark 13:32, Jesus was speaking from the limited perspective of His humanity (see Philip 2:5–11; John 4:6; 19:28). Had He been speaking from His divinity, He would not have said He did not know the hour or day. Many verses show that Christ as God "knows all things" (see John 16:30; Matt 17:27; Luke 5:4–6).

12. Jesus is the Son of God.

Some believe that because Jesus is the Son of God, He must be lesser than God the Father. However, among the ancients, an important meaning of the phrase "son of" is "one who has the same nature as." Jesus as the Son of God has the very nature of God. Jesus' statements, His actions on earth, and His demeanor all demonstrate that He was making Himself equal with God (see John 5:18 NASB; John 10:30 NASB). The Bible clearly states that Jesus existed in the form of God (Philip 2:6 NASB).

13. My Father is greater than I.

What are we to make of Jesus' statements in John 14:28, that "My Father is greater than I"? Simply put, in His humanity, His human state on earth, Christ is lesser than God the Father; but in His deity, He is equal. Biblically, Jesus Christ is *equal* with the Father in His divine nature (John 10:30), but from the standpoint of Him becoming a servant and taking on the likeness of a human, Jesus was positionally then lower than the Father.

14. Jesus is the firstborn.

Some religious cults try to claim that because Jesus is the "first born of creation" (Col 1:15), He is a created being, and therefore cannot be God. Biblically, however, Jesus Christ was not created, but is the *Creator of all things* (Col 1:16; John 1:3). The term *firstborn*, defined biblically, means that Christ is "first in rank" and "preeminent" over the creation that He brought into being. According to Scripture, Jesus *"existed in the form of God"* (Philip 2:5–6 NASB). For He "proceeded forth and came from God" (John 8:42 KJV). At the

Incarnation, the embodiment of God the Son became Jesus Christ as a human being in the flesh (see John 1:14). "Jesus has always been as God is" (Philip 2:6 NLV; John 10:30).

15. What does God say about His Son?

"But God says about His Son, You are God, and you will rule as King forever! Your royal power brings about justice" (Heb 1:8 CEV). The Father declares of Jesus: "But of the Son He says, 'Your throne, O God, is forever and ever, and righteousness is the scepter of your Kingdom" (Heb 1:8 NET).The Father refers to Jesus as "O God," indicating that Jesus is, indeed, God.

16. What does the full image and likeness of God look like?

It looks like Jesus Christ! The Bible specifically states that "Christ is the *exact* likeness of God" (2 Cor 4:4 NLT). "Christ is the visible image of the invisible God" (Col 1:15 NLT).

17. "No prophecy was ever produced by the will of man" (2 Peter 1:21 ESV).

Christ prophesied as only God can, when He stated that His forthcoming resurrection from the dead would vindicate the very special claims that He made for Himself (Matt 12:23–40), and after having been crucified and buried in the tomb of Joseph of Arimathea, Jesus did, in fact, rise from the dead. The resurrection of Christ is an established fact of history and witnessed by many people, including more than five hundred persons at one time (see 1 Cor 15:6). The truth of this miraculous event is very powerful and provides supreme evidence for Christ's divinity.

18. Is Peter very clear in identifying who Jesus Christ is?

Yes! "This letter is from Simon Peter, a slave and apostle of Jesus Christ. I am writing to you who share the same precious faith we have. This faith was given to you because of the justice and fairness of Jesus Christ, *our God and Savior*" (2 Peter 1:1 NLT).

19. Is the Bible very clear in identifying who God is?

Yes, the Holy Bible itself *explicitly* describes Jesus as God in numerous places (See Titus 2:13 KJV; Heb 1:8 KJV; Phil 2:6 NASB; John 10:30 KJV; John 8:24–27 NASB; Matt 1:23 AKJV; Ps 95:6–7 KJV; Ps 100:3 NASB; 1 Cor 1:24 KJV).

20. Who is the radiance and representation of God?

"The Son is the radiance of God's glory and the *exact* representation of His being, sustaining *all* things by His powerful word" (Heb 1:3 NIV). "God's Son shines out with God's glory, and all that God's Son is and does *marks Him as God*" (Heb 1:3 TLB). Yes, as Scripture affirms, "God was manifested in the flesh" (1 Tim 3:16 KJV). "For Christ is not only God-like, He *is God in human flesh*" (see Col 2:9 NLV). "Christ is the power of God *and* the wisdom of God" (1 Cor 1:24 NLT). "Christ was truly God" (Philip 2:6 CEV). Even on Jesus' birth, the Bible *clearly* identifies Him as "the Wonderful Counselor, Mighty God, Eternal Father, Prince of Peace" (Isa 9:6 NASB). And here is His claim to final authority: Christ *Himself* declares, "I am the Alpha and the Omega," says the Lord God, "who is and who was and who is to come, the Almighty" (Rev 1:8 NASB).

21. The Bible is God's infallible Word as proven and validated through hundreds of fulfilled prophecies.

No other book in the world, or other "written religious authority" in all of history, has provided such purity of text, such a high degree of historical and archeological confirmations, and such extensive prophecy fulfilled like the Bible does. It simply does not exist! Therefore, the Bible must be trusted, and Christ must be viewed as God by virtue of all of these overwhelming biblical facts. He has the names of God, the attributes of God, the power of God, and the authority of God. He does the works of God, performs the miracles of God, and is worshiped as God.

O people of Israel and nations of the earth, truly, what more can be said about God's Word and Christ's absolute and divine authority? There can be no misunderstanding as to the meaning of His words. His message is both clear and to the point. To those who still disagree and wish to give greater trust and credence to man and the traditions of religion over Christ and God's very own Words, please, consider what our Lord once said, "You know neither God's Scriptures nor God's power—and so your assumptions are all wrong" (Matt 22:29 voice). "Know that the Son of God has come and has given us an understanding, that we may know Him who is true; in His Son Jesus Christ. *This is the true God* and eternal life" (1 John 5:20 NKJV).

Those who refuse to honor the Son while claiming to honor the Father are actually *self-deceived.* Scripture states, "If we have faith in God's Son, we have believed what God has said. But if we don't believe what God has said about his Son, it is the same as calling God a *liar"* (1 John 5:10 CEV). Let that never be the case. Pray and earnestly ask that God may reveal His will to you and strengthen you according to His Word. He will not force His will upon you. You are always free to choose. But choose truth. Love truth and hunger for it. As Jesus said, "Everyone on the side of truth, sides with Me" (John 18:37). Therefore, side with truth and Christ and seek and ask and pray, and believing, He will help you. He *is* "Our Wonderful Counselor, our Mighty God and our Eternal Father" (Isa 9:6).

CHAPTER 20

What Are the Eternal Effects of *Not* Believing in Jesus Christ?

"Whoever believes in Him [Jesus] is not condemned, but whoever does not believe is condemned already, because he has not believed in the name of the only Son of God" (John 3:18 ESV). "He who believes in the Son *has* eternal life; but he who does not obey the Son will not see life, but the wrath of God abides on him" (John 3:36 NASB). "Who is the liar but the one who denies that Jesus is the Christ?" (1 John 2:22 NASB). "Always think about Jesus Christ" (2 Tim. 2:8 GW). "Fix your thoughts on Jesus" (Heb. 3:1 NIV). Jesus said, "If you love Me, you will keep My commandments" (John 14:15 NASB) "Anyone who does not stay with the teaching of Christ, but goes beyond it, does *not* have God. Whoever does stay with the teaching has both the Father and the Son. So then, if some come to you who do not bring this teaching, do not welcome them in your homes; do not even say, "Peace be with you." For anyone who wishes them peace becomes their partner in the evil things they do" (2 John 9-11 GNT).

Comment: Scripture is absolutely clear; anyone who rejects Jesus Christ condemns himself to eternal punishment! Of *infinitely greater* importance than any church, any religion, or any human testimony is that of the Father who sent Jesus, and God the Father directly attests to Jesus Christ's authority through two events. One happened at the baptism of our Lord when a voice out of heaven said of Him, "You are My Son, whom I love; with you I am well pleased" (Luke 3:22 NIV). The other is at the transfiguration where God our Father speaks out and declares: "This is My Son, My Chosen One; listen to Him!" (Luke 9:35 ESV).

You ask: "Where can we have final authority on God's Word, His will, and His salvation?" Here is the answer: directly from God in heaven: "Listen to Him." God appointed Jesus, marking Him out, holding Him up before us as the last Word, the ultimate truth and authority, the one to whom we are to listen to, pay attention to, and believe. And Jesus did not hesitate to assert His unique authority in *very clear definitive words* when He declared, "I am the vine . . . " (John 15:1-8 NASB). "I am the bread of life" (John 6:35 NASB). "I am the light of the world" (John 8:12 NASB). "I am the good shepherd" (John 10:14 NASB). "I am the resurrection and the life" (John 11:25 NASB). "I am the way, and the truth, and the life" (John 14:6 ESV). "I am the door [to heaven] if anyone enters through Me, he will be saved" (John10:10 NASB). "I am in the Father" (John 14:10,11 NASB). "I am He" (John 8:24,28 NASB). "I am from above" (John 8:23 NASB). "I am the Alpha and the Omega," says the Lord God, "who is and who was and who is to come, the Almighty" (Rev. 1:8 NASB).

We must remember that it is *this* characteristic, personal emphasis that brings Jesus Christ into contrast with all the other prophets! Those Old Testament prophets were mighty men. They were great personalities. But there is not one who ever used this "I." They would all say, "Thus says the Lord," or "The Lord said." But Jesus Christ does not put it like that. He says. "I say to you," or "I am." His whole emphasis is upon "these sayings of *mine*." Not anyone else's.

Here is His claim to final authority. He never once shied away from declaring His authority as sovereign Master. He proclaimed it to His disciples, to His enemies, and to casual inquirers alike, and refusing to tone down or retract the implications of His statements even to His death on the cross. So the true gospel according to Jesus is a message that cannot be separated from the reality of His Lordship. And if it is possible to add to such a statement, He did so when He said; "For truly, I say to you, until heaven and earth pass away, not an iota, not a dot, will pass from the law until all is accomplished" (Matt. 5:18 ESV). Believe in His every word. Believe in His authority. Believe in His power. Jesus said, "I have come as light into the world, so that everyone who believes in Me will not remain in darkness" (John 12:46 NASB).

All these Scriptural words and statements about Jesus Christ are authoritative, descriptive in nature, and very clear in portraying the true and exact meaning of what God wanted conveyed to us. And Jesus affirmed and warned, "You will die in your sins; if you do not believe that I am He, you will die in your sins" (John 8:24 NKJV).

Truly, what more can be said here about Christ's absolute authority? The divine words and statements are crystal clear and leave no misunderstanding. His numerous statements are both explicit and emphatic. To deny His very words and statements and discredit Christ is to side with the devil himself. God asks, "But who are you, a mere man, to criticize and contradict and answer back to God? Will what is formed say to Him that formed it, Why have you made me thus?" (Rom. 9:20 AMPC). Human reasoning cannot be allowed to discredit or distort parts of the Bible to "fit" man's religion or his belief system, nor can the authority of God or any of our Lord's statements be "usurped" by those whom He created! Who are we to ever deny Christ and God's very own words attesting to His chosen one? "For He whom God has sent speaks the words of God" (John 3:34 NKJV). Therefore, the seriousness of such an act of denying Christ, His position, His words, His gospel or His authority cannot be emphasized enough!!

This has grave and eternal consequences for the nonbeliever, and as Scripture warns, "He who believes in Him is not judged; [but] he who does not believe has been judged already, because he has not believed" (John 3:18 NASB). "He who hates Me," Jesus warned, "hates My Father also" (Matt. 15:23 NASB). "He who does not obey the Son will not see life, but the wrath of God abides on Him" (John 3:36 NASB). Those who continue to refuse to honor the Son while claiming to honor the Father are actually self-deceived. The Bible *clearly* says in 1 John 5:10 that to reject Jesus, then, is to call God a liar. Jesus says in John 16:8-9 that this world's sin is that it refuses to believe in Him. We must all come to believe to be saved! "Therefore encourage one another, and build up one another" (1 Thess. 5:11 NASB). "For God has not destined us for wrath, but for obtaining salvation through our Lord Jesus Christ, who died for us, . . . that we may live together with Him" (1 Thess. 5:9-10 NASB).

If your full faith, love, and trust are with the teachings of your religion that run contrary to the teachings of Christ in the Bible, then your religion has a strong "death hold" on you. Turn away from such a religion! God says do not be deceived! Our Lord says listen to *His* voice. "But grow in the grace and knowledge of our Lord and Savior Jesus Christ" (2 Peter 3:18 NASB). "Let the Word of Christ richly dwell within you" (Col. 3:16 NASB). Scripture warns, "See to it that no one takes you captive through philosophy and empty deception, according to the tradition of men, according to the elementary principles of the world, rather than according to Jesus Christ" (Col. 2:8 NASB). "Let no one keep defrauding you of your prize" (Col. 2:18 NASB). Jesus said, "You search the Scriptures, for in them you think you have eternal life; and these are they which testify of Me. But you are not willing to come to Me that you may have life" (John 5:39-40 NKJV).

Unbelievers willfully reject Jesus' testimony to the truth because the Bible says they are "dead in their trespasses and sins" (Eph. 2:1 NASB), and "blinded by Satan" (2 Cor. 4:4 NLT). And those who willfully reject Jesus Christ and blatantly scorn His sacrifice will not do well. "For the wrath of God is revealed from Heaven against all ungodliness and unrighteousness of men who suppress the truth in unrighteousness, because that which is known about God is evident within them; for God made it evident to them. For since the creation of the world His invisible attributes, His eternal power and divine nature, have been clearly seen, being understood through what has been made, so they are without excuse. For even though they knew God, they did not honor Him as God or give thanks, but they became futile in their speculations, and their foolish heart was darkened" (Rom. 1:18-21 NASB). The Bible states, "Just think how much more severe the punishment will be for those who have turned their backs on the Son of God, trampled on the blood of the covenant by which He made holy, and outraged the Spirit of grace with their contempt?" (Heb. 10:28-29 VOICE).

We seriously err to give greater credence and trust to "man" and his "religion" over the very words of Christ and the Bible for our guidance to salvation and God's will. That is absolutely not what God teaches. Scripture warns, "Cursed is the man who trusts in mankind" (Jer. 17:5 NASB). God has clearly pointed out His "chosen one" for us. That is Jesus. Trust Him, listen to Him, God said. We are to have a loving and trusting relationship with Jesus and an unconditional belief in all His statements as spoken in Scripture.

This is important: Jesus is the litmus test of reality for all persons and all religions. He said it so clearly, "And he who rejects Me rejects the One who sent Me" (Luke 10:16 NASB). "Whoever transgresses and does not abide in the doctrine of Christ, does not have God" (2 John 9 NKJV). Jesus Himself said in Revelation 1:8 GNT "I am the first and the last," says the Lord God Almighty, who is, who was, and who is to come. People and religions who reject Christ, reject God and do not know God in a saving way. God has made it clear for the childlike to understand these words. But not all people will understand or perceive the same words. Why? Because Jesus said that they are solely reserved for the "childlike," those with an open mind, those without prejudice, without any preconceived, prepossessed, or biased influence. "God chose things the world considers foolish in order to shame those who think they are wise. And He chose things that are powerless to shame those who are powerful" (1 Cor. 1:27 NLT).

Question: Do you understand who Christ really is and what sends people to eternal punishment? It is not lying, not murder, not stealing, not arson, not rape. It is not sexual perversion, not pride, not arrogance. It is this: unbelief, and the permanent rejection of our Lord and Savior Jesus Christ! It is unbelief and an unrepentant heart that permanently shuts the door to heaven. In the spiritual realm, nothing is possible if you do not believe, but "all things are possible to him who believes" (Mark 9:23 NASB). Just as you live physically by breathing, you live spiritually by faith and belief. As the Bible says, "The just and upright shall live by faith" (Rom. 1:17 AMP). Rejoice, therefore, because if you are a believer, you have a *sure hope* of heaven to enjoy that will be validated for all eternity.

CHAPTER 21

Who Is Our Mediator?
Who Is The Source of Our Salvation?
What's The Gospel of Jesus Christ?

" For there is one God, and one mediator between God and men, the man Christ Jesus; Who gave himself a ransom for all" (1 Tim. 2:5-6 KJV). "And there is salvation in no one else; for there is no other name under heaven that has been given among men by which we must be saved" (Acts 4:12 NASB). All roads may lead to Rome, but all religions do *not* lead to God and salvation. There is only *one* way to salvation, and that is God's way; and God's way is a person, and that person is His Son, the Lord Jesus Christ. Again, God's word says, "Only Jesus has the power to save!" (Acts 4:12 CEV).

"And being made perfect, He became the *source* of eternal salvation to all who obey Him" (Heb. 5:9 ESV). Jesus died on the cross so that you and I could be reconciled to God, no longer counting people's sins against them. "He canceled the record of the charges *against us,* and took it away by nailing it to the cross" (Col. 2:14 NLT). The cross shows the *seriousness* of our sins, but also shows us the *immeasurable love* God has for us. "For God so loved the world, that He gave His only Son, that whoever believes in Him, should not perish but have eternal life" (John 3:16 ESV).

This is the wonderful message of reconciliation He has given us. Therefore, "We implore you on Christ's behalf; *be reconciled to God.* [For our sake] God made Him who had no sin to be sin on our behalf, so that in Him we might become the righteousness of God" (2 Cor. 5:20-21 NIV), because "He gave His life as a ransom for many, [paying the price to set us free from the penalty of sin]" (Matt. 20:28 AMP). "Christ Himself carried our sins in His body to the cross, so that we might die to sin and live for righteousness. It is by His wounds that you have been healed" (1 Peter 2:24 GNT). "For Jesus is the one who leads them to salvation" (Heb. 2:10 GNT). "Because He suffered death for us. Yes, because of God's great kindness, Jesus tasted death for everyone in all the world" (Heb. 2:9 TLB).

"In this is love, not that we loved God, but that He loved us and sent His Son to be the propitiation [that is, the atoning sacrifice, and the satisfying offering] for our sins [fulfilling God's requirement for justice against sin and placating His wrath]. . . . God so loved us [in this incredible way], we also ought to love one another" (1 John 4:10-11 AMP). "He that spared not His own Son, but delivered Him up for us all, how shall He not with Him also freely give us all things?" (Rom. 8:32 AKJV).

"For it is by grace [God's remarkable compassion and favor drawing you to God] that you have been saved [actually delivered from judgment and given eternal life] through faith. And this [salvation] is not of yourselves [not through your own effort], but it is the [undeserved, gracious] gift of God; not as a result of [your] works [nor your attempts to keep the law], so that no one will [be able to] boast or take credit in any way [for his salvation]" (Eph. 2:8-9 AMP).

Question: If Jesus Christ is not your trusted Mediator and Lord and Savior, "Reconciling you to God," then who is? "For [according to God] there is salvation in <u>no one else</u>; for there is no other name under heaven that has been given among men, by which we must be saved" (Acts 4:12 NASB). "Of Him all the prophets bear witness that through His name everyone who believes in Him receives forgiveness of sins" (Acts 10:43 NASB). This is the good news and gospel of Christ. Your eternity with God depends on your willingness to understand and believe the true gospel of Christ. Do not be deceived! "**Watch out!** Don't let evil thoughts or doubts make any of you turn from the living God" (Heb. 3:12 CEV). Scripture affirms "His name is the only one in all the world that can save anyone" (Acts 4:12 CEV).

Comment: The follower of Christ must always remember this very important truth: Eternal security resides *only* in Christ. (See 1 Tim. 2:5-6 NASB, Acts 4:10-12 NASB Matthew 1:21 NASB). There is no side door to heaven! Jesus said, "I am the door; if anyone enters through Me, he shall be saved" (John 10:9 NASB). Apart from Him, there exists no security, no hope, and no everlasting life in heaven. Other religions and philosophies may preach and claim that all roads lead to God, but their contradictory beliefs *cannot* be reconciled.

Trust what your Bible says. Only when we turn to Christ in faith and trust, repenting and seeking His forgiveness, can we be assured of our salvation. But beware: Satan will do *all* in his power through man and false religions to make you think otherwise, to discredit Christ, and to induce doubt in your mind about God's very words in Scripture. As Scripture states: Do not be deceived!!

Remember this: "In Christ," we have power over sin (see 1 John 3:6). If we do stumble, we have an advocate whose blood continually cleanses us as we walk in fellowship with Him (see 1 John 1:7, 1 John 2:1). "In Christ," we are seated in the heavenly places (see Ephesians 2:6). "In Christ," we are rooted, built up, and established in the faith (see Colossians 2:7). "In Christ," we are new creatures (see 2 Cor. 5:17). We have the hope of the glory because we are "in Christ" and Christ is in us (Col. 1:27). "In Christ," we have redemption through His blood (see Eph. 1:7). "In Christ," having also believed, we were sealed in Him (see Eph. 1:13). "In Christ," we possess eternal life (see 1 John 5:11).

Without Christ you can do nothing (see John 15:4-5). It is even said of God's elect in Romans 8:29 NIV: "For those God foreknew He also predestined to be conformed to the Image of His Son." Therefore, if God has predestined our conformity *to Christ*, who then do you think we should follow and side with for truth? Man, religion or Jesus Christ? Jesus said, "Everyone on the side of truth sides with Me" (John 18:37 NIV).

For these reasons, there is no greater stronghold so secure and so sure as the position in Christ for eternal salvation. Remember, God Himself said, "This is My Son, My chosen one; listen to Him" (Luke 9:35 NASB). These are God's clear and divine words of instruction to mankind! "Whoever believes in the Son of God confirms God's testimony. Whoever refuses to believe in effect calls God a liar, refusing to believe God's own testimony regarding His Son" (1 John 5:10 MSG). Therefore, know to whom you are listening to! Turn away from any preacher or religion who refuses to accept God's spoken words and refuses to listen to and abide by the very words of Christ, as God *specifically instructed us to do!* These religions neither represent God nor can they ever save you.

To whom is salvation promised at Christ's appearing? "So Christ, having been offered once *and* once for all to bear [as a burden] the sins of many, will appear a second time [when He returns to earth], not to deal with sin, but to bring salvation to *those who are eagerly and confidently waiting for Him.*" (Hebrews 9:28 AMP).

God said only "the one who believes in the Son of God has the testimony in himself" (1 John 5:10 NASB). Remember, Christ is our mediator, our Savior, and our source of eternal salvation. There is *none* other. "For Jesus is the one who leads them to salvation" (Heb. 2:10 GNT). In reflecting and considering all the loving steps our Lord has taken for mankind, and the great inheritance He has promised to His children, we truly, owe Him an infinite debt of gratitude, and ought never cease giving thanks to Him.

God's Key Points Of Salvation To Remember

Why Was Jesus Born on Earth?

"For this reason I have been born, and for this reason I have come into the world, to bear witness and *testify to the truth*. Everyone who is of the truth hears **My** voice" (John18:37 NASB). Trust Him!

What is The Truth About Man?

"For all have sinned and fall short of the glory of God" (Romans 3:23 NASB). "For the wages of sin is death, but the free Gift of God is Eternal Life through Jesus Christ our Lord" (Romans 6:23 NASB).

How Did God Demonstrate His Love For Us?

"God demonstrates His own love toward us, in that while we were still sinners, Christ died for us" (Romans 5:8 NASB). "He Himself bore our sins in His body on the cross, so that we might die to sin and live for righteousness; for by His wounds you were healed" (1 Peter 2:24 NIV). "In Him we have redemption through His blood, the forgiveness of our trespasses, according to the riches of His grace" (Ephesians 1:7 NASB).

Our Requirement To Receive and Trust Him

"And all who did *receive and trust Him*, He gave **them** the right to be reborn as children of God" (John 1:12 VOICE). "For by grace you have been saved through faith. And this is not your own doing; it is a Gift of God" (Eph. 2:8 ESV). -because you have *received and trusted Him*.

What Did Christ Declare?

"I assure you, most solemnly I tell you, he who believes in Me [who adheres to, trusts in, relies on, and has faith in Me] **has** Eternal Life" (John 6:47 AMPC). "I am the way, the truth and the life. No one comes to the Father except through Me" (John 14:6 NKJV).

What Did Christ Preach?

"If you confess with your mouth Jesus as Lord, and believe in your heart that God raised Him from the dead, you **will** be saved; for with the heart a person believes, resulting in righteousness, and with the mouth he confesses, resulting in salvation" (Romans 10:9-10 NASB), but "Unless you *repent* [turn from your sinful ways and live changed lives], you will all likewise perish" (Luke 13:3 NASB).

What Did Christ Promise Us?

"Truly, truly, I say to you, he who hears *My* Word, and believes Him who sent Me, *has* Eternal life, and does not come into judgement, but has passed out of death into life" (John 5:24 NASB). "He who believes in Him is not condemned; but he who does not believe is condemned already, ...and shall not see life, but the wrath of God abides on him" (John 3:18,36 NKJV).

Why Were These Things Written?

"These things I have written to you who believe in the name of the Son of God, so that you may **know** that you have Eternal Life" (1 John 5:13 NASB).

What Was Promised To All Believers In Christ?

"And you also were included in Christ when you heard the message of truth, the Gospel of your salvation. When you *believed*, you were marked in Him with a seal, the promised Holy Spirit, who is a deposit *guaranteeing your inheritance* until the redemption of those who are God's possession-to the praise of His glory" (Eph. 1:13-14 NIV), "to obtain an inheritance which is imperishable and undefiled and will not fade away, reserved in heaven for you" (1 Peter 1:4 NASB).

CHAPTER 22

If Jesus Christ is the Source of Salvation, What Must We Do to Be Saved?

"If you confess with your mouth Jesus as Lord, and believe in your heart that God raised Him from the dead, you will be saved; for with the heart a person believes, resulting in righteousness, and with the mouth he confesses, resulting in salvation. For the Scripture says, 'Whoever believes in Him, will not be disappointed (Rom. 10:9-11 NASB). "Believe in the Lord Jesus, and you shall be saved, you and your household" (Acts 16:31 NASB). "This precious value then, is for you, who believe" (1 Peter 2:7 NASB).

Comment: Salvation is simply a process of confessing, believing, and *abiding* in the gospel of Christ. A man must confess that Jesus is Lord, which signifies his realization that Christ must have rule over his life with all His righteous requirements. It is by believing in your heart that you are made right with God, and it is by confessing with your mouth that you are saved. Hold fast therefore to the source of all power and eternal life, Jesus Christ, and let the Word of Christ richly dwell within you because "whoever accepts and trusts the Son gets in on *everything.*" (John 3:36 MSG)

Scripture also teaches that no amount of human goodness, human works, or any kind of religious activity can ever gain acceptance with God or get anyone into heaven. The moral man, the religious man, and the immoral and non-religious are *all* in the same boat. They *all* fall short of God's glory and perfect righteousness.

The Bible says, "For it is by God's grace that you have been saved *through faith*. It is not the result of your own efforts, but God's gift, so that no one can boast about it" (Eph. 2:8 GNT). "And this is the testimony, that God gave us eternal life, and this life is in His Son. Whoever has the Son has life; whoever does not have the Son of God does not have life" (1 John 5:11-12 ESV).

Therefore, know that by the Word of God, "He who believes in the Son has eternal life; but he who does not obey the Son shall not see life, but the wrath of God abides on him" (John 3:36 NASB). Remember however, that genuinely believing in Him also means to trust and abide and grow in the knowledge of Him. People who think they just need "believe" to be saved and are then on the high road to heaven are in serious error and *not* saved. In other words, if in their lives there is no change of heart, no change of character, and no evidence by works of the Spirit, do they really have Jesus, or do they only have a head knowledge about Him? As Scripture says "For just as the human body without the spirit is dead, so faith without works [of obedience] is also dead" (James 2:26 AMP).

So what must one do to for salvation? Our Lord said; "He who offers a sacrifice of thanksgiving honors Me; And to him who orders *his way aright*, I shall show the salvation of God" (Psalms 50:23 NASB). "Believe in the Lord Jesus and you shall be saved" (Acts 16:31 NASB).

CHAPTER 23

We Are Instructed to Grow in What and from Whom?

"But grow in the grace and knowledge of our Lord and Savior Jesus Christ" (2 Peter 3:18 NASB). "Therefore, as you received Christ Jesus the Lord, so walk in Him" (Col. 2:6 ESV). Let your roots grow down into Christ, and draw up nourishment *from Him*. See that you go on growing in the Lord, and become strong and vigorous in the truth (Col. 2:7 author paraphrase). Jesus said, "If you abide in My Word [continually obeying My teachings and living in accordance with them], then you are truly My disciples. And you will know the truth [regarding salvation], and the truth will set you free [from the penalty of sin]" (John 8:31-32 AMP). Jesus promises that we shall know the truth and the truth shall set us free. But understand that His promise here is conditional. We gain access to His truth and understanding by believing in *Him* and then *abiding and holding to His teaching*. To say that you believe in the Bible is not enough.

Jesus said, "I am the true vine, and My father is the vinedresser. Every branch in Me that does not bear fruit, He takes away; and every branch that bears fruit, He prunes it, that it may bear more fruit. Abide in Me, and I in you. As the branch *cannot* bear fruit of itself, unless it abides in the vine, so neither can you, *unless* you abide in Me. I am the vine, you are the branches; he who abides in Me, and I in him, he bears much fruit; for apart from Me you can do nothing. If anyone does not abide in Me, he is thrown away as a branch, and dries up; and they gather them, and cast them into the fire, and they are burned. If you abide in Me, and My words abide in you, ask whatever you wish, and it shall be done for you. If you keep My commandments, you will abide in My love. . . . These things I have spoken to you, that My joy may be in you, and that your joy may be made full" (John 15:1-2, 4-7, 10-11 NASB).

Comment: As long as Satan has the power to deceive, he will deceive people, and they in turn will try to deceive you. The worst kind of deceiver is the false teacher, who appears to give good advice but actually will lead you down a path to eternal destruction. If someone is trying to convince you to do something or believe something that contradicts the very truth in Scripture or the authority in Christ, you can be assured it is wrong.

Know the Bible well enough to know the truth and discern when someone is telling you something false. Do not lose your eternal salvation for lack of biblical knowledge, or for having a greater faith and trust in man and his religion than in Christ and the Bible. Do not make this fatal and eternal mistake. "Trust in the Lord with all your heart and lean not on your own understanding" (Prov. 3:5 NIV). As Scripture instructs, "Now stay focused on Jesus, who designed and perfected our faith" (Heb. 12:2 VOICE).

CHAPTER 24

What *Specifically* Are We Told about the Gospel of Christ?

" For I am not ashamed of the gospel, for it is the power of God for salvation to everyone who believes" (Rom. 1:16 NASB). "Therefore do not be ashamed of the testimony of our Lord, who abolished death and brought life and immortality to light through the gospel" (2 Tim. 1:8, 10 NKJV). And Jesus said: "Go throughout the whole world and preach the gospel to all people" (Mark 16:15 GNT). "You see, in the good news, God's restorative justice is revealed. And as we will see, it begins with and ends in faith. As the Scripture declares, 'By faith the just will obtain life'" (Rom. 1:17 VOICE). Why was this Gospel written? The Bible states in the Gospel of John that "These are written so that you may believe that Jesus is the Christ, the Son of God. Then, by believing, you may have life through His name" (John 20:31 NCV).

Comment: In summary, the gospel is the good news that God is restoring our broken lives through the death and resurrection of Jesus Christ. It is clear that the gospel of Christ is the power of salvation to everyone who *believes*. But it has a contingency! The Gospel of Christ is the power of God for salvation *only* when you *believe*!

God's word's of instruction and His message are very clear. Yet Satan the devil is quietly diverting our attention from God's core message in the Bible. Instead of preaching and abiding by the Good News that sinners can be made righteous in Christ and escape the wrath to come, some religions have come to accept and preach a different and false version of the gospel that implies that God's main purpose in saving us is to lay out a wonderful plan for our lives, a plan that brings us peace and happiness, all without a word about the law, repentance, or the consequence of sin and disbelief! This message is erroneous and misleading.

Churches that are overemphasizing any one of God's attributes to the exclusion of others can lead to heresy. In other words, teaching only about God's great love and mercy without the law, without repentance, without convicting of sin or without Christ is not Biblical. It also prevents people from understanding God's hatred of sin and the future punishment for wrong doing. By emphasizing and presenting God only as "loving", and not teaching the law or the *consequence* of sin, we present a distorted view of God and this prevents people from seeing their real need for a Savior.

It is impossible for a person to fully realize his need for God's grace until he see's how terribly he has failed the standards of God's Law. It also lowers the relevance of God's law and dims the light by which man perceives his guilt. For this reason, almost everyone today thinks they are headed for Heaven because they "feel" they are morally good. The Bible tells us in (Proverbs 20:6) that "most men will proclaim each his own goodness." Why? Because they don't have a *true* definition of "good". As Paul an apostle of Christ explained: "I would not have known sin except through the law" [The Commandments] (Rom. 7:7 NASB). The thing that primes the sinners ear to hear the voice of the Son of God is the Law. It is the Law that converts the soul, so that the person becomes a new creation in Christ (see 2 Corin. 5:17). "Therefore the Law has become our tutor *to lead us* to Christ, that we may be justified by faith" (Gal. 3:24 NASB).

When a sinner understands the horrific consequences of breaking God's Law, he will flee to the Savior in genuine repentance, solely to escape the wrath that is to come. "God is now declaring to men that all people everywhere should repent, because He has fixed a day in which He will judge the world in righteousness" (Acts 17:30-31 NASB). The issue is not one of peace and happiness but one of *righteousness*. Scripture states, "The Law of the Lord is perfect, converting the soul; the commandment of the Lord is pure, enlightening the eyes. ...Moreover by them is thy servant warned: and in keeping of them *there is great reward* (Psalms 19:7-11 AKJV). Make it a point therefore to know God's law and the true gospel of Christ in your Bible.

Your faith and trust in Jesus Christ and His statements release the power of God that saves you. But you *must* believe. The gospel of Christ is the power of God for salvation to everyone who *believes*.

Beware: As Scripture has forewarned, in this age, false gospels of carnal Christianity are rampant and they have deceived and continue to deceive many followers. Today there are many Christian religions and denominations that do not bow to the lordship of Jesus Christ, and deny both His authority and words in Scripture. The reason this false gospel of carnal Christianity has been so widespread and so widely received is because it makes no demands upon you. It gives only a "form of godliness," like a covering, which allows its converts to indulge in any sin enumerated in 2 Timothy 3:2-4, and yet claim they are saved and on the high road to heaven!

Why are so many people deceived today concerning God's way to salvation? Because they do not know that regeneration is *imperative*. Our Creator made this clear when He said, "I assure you and most solemnly I say to you, unless a person is born again [reborn from above, spiritually transformed, renewed and sanctified], he cannot [ever] see and experience the kingdom of God" (John 3:3 AMP).

This leads us to an important question for review! What two key steps are required to begin this important regeneration process Jesus declared was so necessary for salvation? Can you name them? The answer. First: As Scripture states, believe and abide in the *Biblical* gospel of Christ, for it is the only gospel that contains the power of God for salvation when you *believe*. It is "By faith the just will obtain life" (Rom. 1:17 VOICE). Jesus said, Truly, truly, I say to you, he who hears My word, and believes Him who sent Me, has eternal life" (John 5:24 NASB). Second: God's laws and holiness demands eternal consequences for sin, and His anger over sin should never be underestimated. "Repent therefore and be converted, that your sins may be blotted out" (Acts 3:19).

Jesus proclaimed, "but unless you repent [change your old way of thinking, turn from your sinful ways and live changed lives], you will all likewise perish" (Luke 13:3 AMP). We cannot be "converted" unless we repent. That is why Jesus commanded that *repentance* be preached to all nations (Luke 24:47). Turn away from religions that preach a gospel message contrary to the gospel of Christ, as they cannot save you. Don't be deceived! Don't lose out on eternal salvation!

CHAPTER 25

Is the Gospel Veiled and Has Satan Blindfolded This World Spiritually?

"And even if our gospel is veiled [hidden], it is veiled to those who are perishing" (2 Cor. 4:3 NASB). "For the god of this world has blinded the unbelievers' minds [that they should not discern the truth], preventing them from seeing the illuminating light of the gospel of the glory of Christ (the Messiah), who is the image *and* likeness of God" (2 Cor. 4:4 AMPC).

Comment: The god of this world is Satan the devil. He is the father of lies and the master of deception, and has many tricks to try to divert people from receiving the truth about God and salvation. One of his diabolical plots is to pervert God's way by using compromised preaching. False prophets often water down God's Word and mix it with self-centered man-pleasing religious doctrines to lure and seduce people to their religion.

As Scripture says, "For people will be lovers of themselves, lovers of money, boasters, proud, abusive, disobedient to parents, unthankful, unholy, without love, unforgiving, without self-control, brutal, not lovers of the good, conceited, lovers of pleasure rather than lovers of God, having a 'form' of godliness but denying its power" (2 Tim. 3:2-5

NIV). For these reasons and lack of obedience to God's Word, the gospel is veiled to those who are perishing, whose minds the god of this world has blinded, who do not believe, lest the light of the gospel of the glory of Christ should shine on them.

Question: Exactly when does God take away this veil? Up next!

CHAPTER 26

If the Gospel of Christ is Veiled to Unbelievers, Specifically When Does God Take Away the Veil?

"But whenever a person turns [in repentance] to the Lord, the veil is stripped off and taken away" (2 Cor. 3:16 AMPC).

Comment: Here is God's answer! Here's the *key* requirement for us. We must *turn* to the Lord. As Scripture says, "But grow in the grace and knowledge of our Lord and Savior Jesus Christ" (2 Peter 3:18 NASB). "Let your roots grow down into Him [Christ] and draw up nourishment from Him" (Col. 2:7 TLB). Note that God did not say that religion is your life source. Rather, Christ is your life source from which to draw up nourishment. "See that you go on growing in the Lord and become strong and vigorous in the truth" (Col. 2:7 author paraphrase).

Jesus said, "If you abide in My Word [continually obeying My teachings and living in accordance with them], then, you will know the truth [regarding salvation], and the truth will set you free [from the penalty of sin]" (John 8:31-32 AMP).

Remember what Jesus' said: He is the vine and you are the branch and apart from Him, you can do nothing (see John 15:1-5 NASB). You must therefore "respond" to His calling by abiding in His Word. You must *genuinely* believe in His authority and the gospel of Christ. *Then,*

He will remove the spiritual blindfold. Don't allow man and religion to override God's instruction to you. As Scripture warns, do not lean on your own understanding or anyone's belief that would discredit or devalue Christ's authority and His statements. Do not make that mistake and lose out on God's promise and blessings of removing the veil. It is more prudent to trust in our Lord than to lose out on eternal salvation because you give greater credence to man and religion over Christ and the Bible.

Pray as the psalmist pleaded, "Father, Open my eyes to see the wonderful truths in your instruction" (Ps. 119:18 NLT). "Give me understanding, that I may learn your commandments" (Ps. 119:73 NASB). "Yield now and be at peace with Him" (Job 22:21 NASB).

Jesus is the vine and we are the branches. "If those branches that have been cut from the tree do not stay in unbelief, then God will carefully 'graft them back' into the tree because He has the power to do that" (Rom. 11:23 VOICE). Remember, all these statements convey a conditional promise from our loving Creator!

CHAPTER 27

God Emphasized a Certain Part of the Bible, Its Message Is So Important, We Should Do What With It?

"And Jesus came up and spoke to them, saying, All authority has been given to Me in heaven and on earth. Go therefore and make disciples of all the nations, baptizing them in the name of the Father and the Son and the Holy Spirit, teaching them to observe all that I commanded you; And behold, I am with you always, even to the end of the age" (Matt. 28:18-20 NASB). "And He said to them, Go into all the world and proclaim the Gospel to the whole creation. Whoever *believes* and is baptized will be saved; but whoever does not believe will be condemned" (Mark 16:15-16 ESV). "For whoever would save his life will lose it, but whoever loses his life for My sake and the Gospel's will save it" (Mark 8:35 ESV).

"Only conduct yourselves in a manner worthy of the Gospel of Christ" (Phil. 1:27 NASB). "Sing to the Lord, bless His name; Proclaim the good news of His Salvation from day to day" (Ps. 96:2 NKJV). "For it is the power of God for salvation to everyone who believes" (Rom. 1:16 NASB). "For what does it profit a man to gain the whole world, and forfeit his soul?" (Mark 8:36 NASB). "The time is fulfilled, and the kingdom of God is at hand; repent and believe in the Gospel" (Mark 1:15

NASB). "Truly, truly, I say to you, he who hears My word, and *believes* Him who sent Me, has eternal life, and does not come into judgment, but has passed out of death into life" (John 5:24 NASB). "To you it has been given to know the mystery of the Kingdom of God" (Mark 4:11 NKJV). "I write these things to you *who* believe in the name of the Son of God, that you may KNOW that you have eternal life" (1 John 5:13 ESV).

Comment: The gospel is defined and revealed in the Bible, the Word of God, and is the central message of the Holy Scriptures. It is our heavenly Father's plan for the salvation of His children. It is called the gospel of Christ because the atonement of Christ is central to this plan and what Christ accomplished for *you*. *There is no alternate*, and to change its substance (as some religions do) is to pervert and indeed poison and destroy it. The reason why the gospel of Christ is so critically important and singled out by God to be proclaimed throughout the world, is that it gives mankind the life-saving knowledge and way to eternal salvation.

For this very reason, we cannot be disengaged or disinterested in this subject, for it has serious *eternal* ramifications. It is therefore absolutely critical that we make sure, very sure, that we have heard and responded to the *true* gospel of Christ, lest we have a false hope concerning a salvation that we think we may have.

We must be capable of distinguishing false gospels from the real thing. This is important because contrary to Scriptural warnings, many of today's religions and teachers of Christianity have brazenly perverted the gospel of Christ and His message of salvation. So what part of the Bible is so important? The answer is the Gospel. And what are we commanded to do with it? Believe in it and go into the world and proclaim it to the whole creation. Why? Because it gives mankind the life-saving knowledge and way to eternal salvation. How? "For it is the power of God for salvation to everyone who believes" (Rom. 1:16 NASB).

Part 4

Scriptural Summary Points to Remember

- God and His Word accord all divine honors and Full Authority to Jesus Christ.

- God is explicit in commanding that we are to listen to and believe in His Son.

- God sent His Son, Jesus, to bear witness and "testify to the truth" about God's message. Jesus said, "I speak just as the Father had told me." What more authoritative person can anyone have on the face of this earth other than the Son of God?

- He who does not honor the Son does not honor the Father who sent Him. Jesus said, "He who rejects Me, also rejects God who sent Me. I and the Father are one."

- Christ is the *only* source of eternal salvation to all who *believe* and *obey* Him.

- As Scripture instructs, now stay focused on Christ, who designed and perfected our faith.

- God said, "Only Jesus has the power to save" (Acts 4:12 CEV).

- We are to grow in the grace and knowledge of our Lord and Savior Jesus Christ, and let our roots grow down into Him, and draw up nourishment from Him.

- We are to repent and believe in the gospel of Christ, as it is the power of God for salvation to all who believe. Therefore, make sure your listening to the *right* gospel!

- There are grave and eternal consequences for the nonbeliever.

- Turn away from religions that reject the gospel of Christ and Word of God.

- Whoever believes in the Son of God confirms God's testimony. Whoever refuses to believe in effect calls God a liar, refusing to believe God's own testimony regarding His Son.

- The gospel is veiled to unbelievers. When a person *genuinely turns* to the Lord, the veil is stripped away.

- Believe in the Lord Jesus, and you will be saved, you will not be disappointed.

- Jesus is called: "The Image of the Invisible God," "The Wonderful Counselor," "The Mighty God," "The Eternal Father," "The Prince of Peace," "The Everlasting Father," "The King of Kings," "The Holy One."

- Whom did Christ claim to be? "I am the Alpha and the Omega," says the *Lord God*, "who is and who was and who is to come, the Almighty.

PART 5

God's Loving Promises to Believers

CHAPTER 28

What Has God Granted You Pertaining to Life and His Promises?

"His divine power has given us *everything* we need for a godly life through our knowledge of Him who called us by His own glory and goodness. Through these He has given us His very great and precious promises, so that through them you may participate in the divine nature, having escaped the corruption in the world caused by evil desires" (2 Peter 1:3-4 NIV).

"For this very reason, make *every* effort to add to your faith goodness; and to goodness, knowledge, and to knowledge, self-control; and to self-control, perseverance; and to perseverance, godliness; and to godliness, mutual affection; and to mutual affection, love. For if you possess these qualities in increasing measure, they will keep you from being ineffective and unproductive in your knowledge of our Lord Jesus Christ" (2 Peter 1:5-8 NIV).

"Therefore, believers, be all the more diligent to make certain about His calling and choosing you [be sure that your behavior reflects and confirms your relationship with God]; for by doing these things [actively developing these virtues], you will never stumble [in your spiritual growth and will live a life that leads others away from sin]" (2 Peter 1:10 AMP). Remember, Jesus gave up everything so you could have everything you need. He suffered and died so you can live and have eternal life in heaven with Him. That alone is more than worthy of your thanks and appreciation for what He has done for us. Never should we wonder what to be thankful for. For all God has granted us, let us be forever grateful and worship God in a way that will please Him. "Love the Lord your God with all your heart and with all your soul and with all your mind and with all your strength" (Mark 12:30 NIV).

There is nothing, absolutely nothing more important than developing a friendship with God. It's a relationship that will last forever. As Paul told Timothy in Scripture, "Some of these people have missed the most important thing in life - they don't know God. May God's mercy be upon you" (1 Tim. 6:21 TLB). Yet the real truth is, you are as close to God as you choose to be. Close friendship with God is a choice, not an accident. We must intentionally seek it. Do you really want it? What is it worth to you? Do you really know what you are missing?

God wants to be your best friend. He said, "When you get serious about finding Me and want it more than anything else, I'll make *sure* you won't be disappointed" (Jer. 29:13 MSG). Will you make pleasing God the goal of your life? There is nothing that God won't do for the person totally absorbed in doing this.

CHAPTER 29

Exactly What Precious and Magnificent Promises Has God Conditionally Granted You?

"For in this way, the entrance into the eternal Kingdom of our Lord and Savior Jesus Christ will be abundantly supplied to you" (2 Peter 1:11 NASB). "Blessed be the God and Father of our Lord Jesus Christ, who according to His great mercy has caused us to be born again to a living hope through the resurrection of Jesus Christ from the dead, to obtain an inheritance which is imperishable and undefiled, and will not fade away, reserved in heaven for you, who are protected by the power of God through faith, for a salvation ready to be revealed in the last time" (1 Peter 1:3-5 NASB). "THINGS WHICH THE EYE HAS NOT SEEN AND THE EAR HAS NOT HEARD, AND WHICH HAVE NOT ENTERED THE HEART OF MAN, ALL THAT GOD HAS PREPARED FOR THOSE WHO LOVE HIM [who hold Him in affectionate reverence, who obey Him, and who gratefully recognize the benefits that He has bestowed]" (1 Corin. 2:9 AMP). I want you to realize what is the hope of His calling and what are the rich and glorious inheritance God has promised His people (Eph. 1:18 author paraphrase).

"Then the king will say to those on the right, "Come, you who are blessed by My Father; take your inheritance, the kingdom prepared for you since the creation of the world" (Matt. 25:34 NIV). "In this you [should] greatly rejoice" (1 Peter 1:6 NASB). Why? "For obtaining as the outcome of your faith the salvation of your souls" (1 Peter 1:9 NASB). "Do you see what we've got? An unshakable kingdom! And do you see how thankful we must be? No only thankful, but brimming with worship, deeply reverent before God" (Heb. 12:28 MSG).

Other Magnificent Promises God Has Granted You

- I am with you always, even to the end of the world (Matt.28:20 KJV).

- I will *never* leave you *nor* forsake you (Heb. 13:5 NKJV).

- Draw near to God and He will draw near to you (James 4:8 NASB).

- God cannot lie (Titus 1:2 NASB).

- He cares for you (see 1 Peter 5:7 NASB).

- Jesus said, Now that you know [the things I've taught you], you will be blessed if you do them (John 13:17 NIV). The one who looks intently at the perfect law, and abides by it, not having become a forgetful hearer but an effectual doer, *this* man shall be blessed in what he does (James 1:25 NASB).

- Nothing shall separate us from the love of God, which is in Christ Jesus our Lord (Rom. 8:39 NASB).

- [God] The Father has qualified us to share in the inheritance of the saints (Col. 1:12 ESV).

- In Him you also, when you heard the Word of truth, the Gospel of your salvation, and believed in Him [Christ], were sealed with the promised Holy Spirit, who is the guarantee of our inheritance until we acquire possession of it, to the praise of His glory (Eph. 1:13-14 ESV).

- And indeed, all who live godly in Christ will be persecuted (2 Tim. 3:12 NASB). Rejoice and be glad, for your reward in heaven is great! In God's economy we are *blessed* when persecuted. (Matt. 5:10-12 NASB)

- God is faithful and will sanctify you (See 1 Thess. 5:24 NASB).

- For the wages of sin is death, but the free gift of God is eternal life in Christ Jesus our Lord (Romans 6:23 NASB).

- For God so loved the world, that He gave His only begotton Son, that whoever believes in Him should not perish, but have eternal life (John 3:16 NASB).

- And to wait for His Son from heaven... that is Jesus, who delivers us from the wrath to come (1 Thessalonians 1:10 NASB).

- For I know the plans I have for you, says the Lord. They are plans for good and not for disaster, to give you a future and a hope (Jer. 29:11 NLT).

- When you get serious about finding Me and want it more than anything else, I'll make sure you won't be disappointed (Jer. 29:13 MSG).

If you are in Christ, and he is in you, these promises are all yours!

CHAPTER 30

Why Were These Things Written to Those Who Believe, and What Specific Gift Has God Promised His Believers?

"These things I have written to you who believe in the name of the Son of God, so that you may *know* that you have eternal life" (1 John 5:13 NKJV).

"In Him, you also, after listening to the message of truth, the gospel of your salvation, having also believed, you were sealed in Him with the Holy Spirit of promise" (Eph. 1:13 NASB), "who is the guarantee of our inheritance until the redemption of the purchased possession, to the praise of His glory" (Eph. 1:14 NKJV). "You are from God, little children, and have conquered them, because the one who is in you is **greater** than the one who is in the world. They are from the world; therefore they speak from the world's perspective and the world listens to them. We are from God; the person who knows God listens to us, but whoever is not from God does not listen to us. By **this** we know the Spirit of truth and the spirit of deceit" (1 John 4:4-6 NET).

"Don't be afraid, for I am with you. Don't be discouraged, for I am your God. I will strengthen you and help you. I will hold you up with my victorious right hand" (Isa. 41:10 NLT). "Keep your life free from love of money, and be content with what you have, for He has said, I will never leave you nor forsake you" (Heb. 13:5 ESV).

Comment: There is no cause for any faithful Christian to worry and quiver in a state of insecurity. If we truly believe and abide in Him through faith, keeping ourselves in the love of Christ, our eternal future is *secure*.

However, that security does not release us of our God-given responsibilities towards others. God is at work in this world and He wants His faithful servants to join Him. Being a Christian includes being sent into the world as a representative of Christ Jesus.

Jesus said "As the Father has sent Me, I am sending you" (John 20:21 NIV). "Our Creator God has pursued us and brought us into a restored and healthy relationship with Him through the Anointed. And He has given us the same mission, the ministry of reconciliation, to bring others back to Him" (2 Cor. 5:18 VOICE). "He charges us to proclaim the message that heals and restores our broken relationships with God and each other" (2 Cor. 5:19 VOICE).

"So we have been sent to speak for Christ" (2 Cor. 5:20 NCV). "And teach them to do everything I have told you" (Matt. 28:20 CEV). "You must warn [unbelievers] so they may live. If you don't speak out to warn the wicked to stop their evil ways, they will die in their sin" says the Lord (Ezek. 3:18 NCV).

Our mission has eternal significance. Nothing else we do will ever matter as much as helping other people establish an eternal relationship with God. Telling others how they can have eternal life is the greatest thing we can do for them. We *all* need Jesus. Jesus said, "Most assuredly, I say to you, He who believes in Me has everlasting life" (John 6:47 NKJV).

In reviewing this chapter, why were these things written and what specific gift has God promised His believers? Once again here is the answer. "These things I have written to you who believe in the name of the Son of God, so that you may **know**, (while still alive), that you have eternal life! This world is not our home, we are looking forward to our everlasting home in heaven with Jesus. "For our citizenship is in heaven, from which also we eagerly wait for a Savior, the Lord Jesus Christ; who will transform the body of our humble state into conformity with the body of His glory, by the exertion of the power that He has even to subject all things to Himself" (Philip. 3:20-21 NASB). Measured against eternity, our time on earth is but a blink of an eye, but the consequences of it will last forever! The deeds of this short life are the destiny of the next.

PART 6

Sin, Separation, Prayer, and God's Forgiveness

CHAPTER 31

What Exactly Is Sin?

"Everyone who makes a practice of sinning also practices lawlessness; and sin is lawlessness" (1 John 3:4 NASB). "Truly, truly, I say to you, everyone who commits sin is a *slave* to sin" (John 8:34 NASB). It is impossible to deny the existence of sin, when the whole world is in conflict between good and evil. If sin were not a fact we would not need police, there would be no crime, we would not need jails or prisons or locks on doors. "All unrighteousness is sin" (1 John 5:17 KJV). "For all have sinned and fall short of the glory of God" (Rom. 3:23 ESV). Unbelief is sin. "The one who does not believe God has made Him a liar, because he has not believed in the testimony that God has given concerning His Son" (1 John 5:10 NASB; see also John 16:8-9, NASB).

Listen, O heavens and earth: for the Lord hath spoken, sin is a *rebellious act* against God (Isa. 1:2 author paraphrase). "Cry loudly, do not hold back; Raise your voice like a trumpet, and declare to My people their transgressions" (Isa. 58:1 NASB). "Transgressing and denying the Lord, and turning away from our God, speaking oppression and revolt, conceiving in and uttering from the heart lying words" (Isa. 59:13 NASB).

You must warn them so they may live. If you don't speak out to warn the wicked to stop their ways, they will die in their sin. But I will hold you responsible for their death" (Ezek. 3:18 NCV). "But the Scripture says that the whole world is under the power of sin; and so the gift which is promised on the basis of faith in Jesus Christ, is given to those who *believe*" (Gal. 3:22 GNT). "For if we go on sinning willfully after receiving the knowledge of truth, there no longer remains a sacrifice for our sins, but a terrifying expectation of judgment, and the fury of a fire which will consume the adversaries" (Heb. 10:26-27 NASB). "For by your words you will be acquitted, and by your words you will be condemned" (Matt. 12:37, NIV). "No one who is born of God will continue to sin, because God's seed remains in them; they cannot go on sinning, because they have been born of God" (1 John 3:9 NIV).

Comment: Through the knowledge of the law we become conscious of sin. Sin is a folly to deceive you, a force to destroy you, and a fact to condemn you. Sin is a willful act of disobedience against the revealed will of God. Galatians 5:19-21 constitutes the most serious warnings to those who may think they can sin that grace may abound. The influence of sin touches everybody, the innocent as well as the guilty. Sin is so serious it sent Jesus to the cross.

Know that God can break the chain of every sin that binds us if we are sincerely willing to give it up. God comes into our heart and gives us power to change and to overcome sin. Sinners are forgiven when we repent and believe in Jesus. We make a mockery of God's forgiveness when we deliberately and continually engage in sin because we think that God will just forgive us later. God's judgment by the great flood and the destruction of Sodom and Gomorrah are set forth as a *warning* to all sinners today (see 2 Peter 2:4-10, Jude 6-7,14-15, 1 Cor. 10:11-12).

The unpardonable sin is an unrepentant heart and the complete and permanent rejection of our Lord and Savior Jesus Christ.

CHAPTER 32

What Causes a Separation from God?

"Behold, the Lord's hand is not so shortened, that it cannot save, or his ear so dull that it cannot hear; but your iniquities [sins] have made a separation between you and your God, and your sins have hidden his face from you so that he does not hear" (Isa. 59:1-2 ESV). "He who turns away his ear from hearing the law [of God and man], even his prayer is an abomination, hateful and revolting [to God]" (Prov. 28:9 AMPC). The result of sin is separation and death. "Sin came into the world through one man, and his sin brought death with it. As a result, death has spread to the whole human race because everyone has sinned" (Rom. 5:12 GNT). "For the wages of sin is death, but the free gift of God is eternal life in Christ Jesus our Lord." (Rom. 6:23 ESV).

Comment: What causes separation from God that means He does not hear us is sin. And Satan knows how to use sin in a believers life to alienate him from God, confuse him, and create a host of destructive measures for both him and his family, and if he succeeds, deception goes into high gear. Adam and Eve died spiritually the very same day they disobeyed God and ate the fruit. They were literally separated from the presence of God in the garden by being banished from the garden. Paul in the Scriptures describes it as being "alienated" from the life of

God. "For their [moral] understanding is darkened *and* their reasoning is clouded; [they are] alienated *and* self-banished from the life of God [with no share in it; this is] because of the [willful] ignorance *and* spiritual blindness that is [deep-seated] within them, because of the hardness *and* insensitivity of their heart" (Eph. 4:18 AMP).

We are alienated from God. Outside of Christ we are at odds with God. But God calls us to work out our salvation in every area of our life, and we are not alone in this. God enables us to do so. He has given us all we need for life and godliness through Jesus Christ. "Once you were alienated from God and were enemies in your minds because of your evil behavior. But now he has reconciled you by Christ's physical body through death, to present you holy in his sight, without blemish, and free from accusation" (Col. 1:21-22 NIV). "At that time you were apart from Christ. You were foreigners and did not belong to God's chosen people. You had no part in the covenants, which were based on God's promises to his people, and you lived in this world without hope and without God. But now, in *union* with Christ Jesus you, who used to be far away, have been brought near by the blood of Christ" (Eph. 2:12-13 GNT).

Jesus said "I am the door; if anyone enters through Me, he shall be saved. I came that they might have life, and might have it abundantly" (John 10:9,10 NASB). "God is able to make all grace abound to you, so that having all sufficiency in all things at all times, you may abound in every good work" (2 Cor. 9:8 ESV). "For as you [come to] know Him better, He *will* give you, through His great power, everything you need for living" (2 Peter 1:3 TLB). "But *grow* in the grace and knowledge of our Lord and Savior Jesus Christ. To Him *be* the glory, both now and to the day of eternity, Amen" (2 Peter 3:18 NASB).

Remember, sin separates us from God, darkens our understanding and clouds our reasoning, but "If we confess our sins and repent, He is faithful and just to forgive us our sins, and to cleanse us from all un-righteousness" (1 John 1:9 KJV). "God removes our sins from us as far as the east is from the west and He washes us whiter than snow" (Psalm 103:12, 51:7).

CHAPTER 33

What Important Facts Is God Telling Us about Prayer?

"Thus says the Lord who made *the earth*, the Lord who formed it to establish it . . . He explicitly says: "Call to Me and I will answer you, and I will tell you great and mighty things, which you do not know" (Jer. 33:3 NASB). Prayer puts God in the matter with commanding force! We are charged in God's Word: "Always to pray" (see Luke 18:1 ESV), "pray without ceasing" (see 1 Thess. 5:17,NKJV), "Don't worry about anything; instead, Pray about everything; tell God your needs, don't forget to thank him for his answers" (Phil. 4:6 TLB), "Devoted to prayer" (see Rom. 12:12 NASB), "Pray everywhere . . . and without doubting" (1 Tim. 2:8 NKJV), "Pray at all times . . . and with all perseverance" (Eph. 6:18 NASB), "Pray for one another" (James 5:16 ESV), "The effectual fervent prayer of a righteous man availeth [accomplishes] much" (James 5:16 KJV).

Prayer can unlock the treasure chest of God's wisdom (James 1:5 author paraphrase), Because it is a sin not to pray (see 1 Sam. 12:23). "Because sinners can be saved when they pray in faith" (Rom. 10:9-13 author paraphrase). "Pray lest ye enter into temptation" (Luke 22:46 KJV). "Believing, ask in prayer" (Matt. 21:22 KJV). "And when you are praying, do not use meaningless repetition . . . for they suppose that they'll be heard for their many words. So do not be like them; for your Father knows what you need *before* you ask Him" (Matt. 6:7-8 NASB).

Comment: What clear and commanding statements those are that were put in the divine record to provide us with a sure basis of faith and to encourage us to pray! They stress the importance and the absolute necessity of prayer and putting emphasis on its all-prevailing power. The apostles were men of prayer. They gave themselves to prayer. The seed of God's Word (the Bible) must also be saturated in prayer to make it germinate. It (faith) grows more readily and anchors more deeply when it is soaked with prayer. God says, "Never stop praying" (1 Thess. 5:17 NLT).

Always pray to have eyes that see the best in people, a heart that forgives the worst, a mind that forgets the bad, and a soul that never loses faith in God. Know that prayer is a tremendous force in the world. Praying that influences God is said to be the outpouring of the fervent, effectual righteous man. It is prayer on fire. It does not have a weak and flickering light, but shines with a vigorous and steady glow. But heaven has listening ears only to the wholehearted and deeply earnest. Belief, trust and perseverance must back the prayers that Heaven respects and that our Lord hears. Prayer needs no proof other than its accomplishments. Prayer honors God, acknowledges His being, exalts His power, and secures His aid. According to Hebrews 4:16 in the Bible, prayer is the means that God has appointed for our *receiving mercy* and *finding grace* to help in time of need.

But behind the praying, certain conditions of prayer *must* be met. If you want prayers to be powerful and answered you need to become a child of God. In order to be a child of God you must receive and believe in the Lord Jesus Christ as your personal Savior. Have you done this? Does Jesus really, truly, genuinely live in your heart? Our trust and position in Christ must be firm! Once we are born again by God's

Spirit because of our faith and trust and that we repent of our sins, His Spirit comes to permanently indwell us, and His sovereign love placed us in Christ. Scripture says "By His doing you are in Christ Jesus" (1 Corin. 1:30 NASB). Therefore, to have prayers heard and answered, man must make the right choice and side with Christ, God's greatest witness! As the Bible teaches "Only conduct yourselves in a manner worthy of the gospel of *Christ*" (Philip. 1:27 NASB). People just praying in faith without the due honor, respect, trust and belief of the gospel of Christ is not the recipe for prayers to be answered nor fortifying one's heart with truth and receiving God's blessings. Christ was God's witness and *His* testimony *must* be accepted for prayer to prevail. Too many hear the word and understand or claim to understand. But God does not want just that! We are told "But be ye doers of the word, and not hearers only, deceiving your own selves" (James 1:22 KJV). "We please God by what we *do*, and not only by what we believe" (James 2:24 CEV).

Another hinderance to prayer is explained in God's book the Bible that declares, "Listen! The Lord's arm is not too weak to save you, nor is his ear too deaf to hear you call. It is *your sins* that have cut you off from God. Because of your sins, He has turned away and will not listen anymore" (Isa. 59:1-2 NLT). One of the most awful things about sin and un-repented sin is the way it hinders prayer. It severs the connection between us and the source of all grace and power and blessings. Anyone who desires power in prayer must be merciless in dealing with his own sins. And I myself am not without sin. But as long as we hold on to sin or have any controversy with God, we cannot expect Him to heed our prayers. Harboring a sin is different from committing a sin. Harboring a sin means knowing about a sin thats present, knowing God has an eye on it, and still not settling it. It does affect us! Harbored sin is like static on a radio. Because of it we faintly hear God's voice, but we can't make it right.

It's not that He cannot hear you; it's that sin has come between you and our Holy God. The Bible says "We know that God does not hear sinners; but if anyone is God-fearing, and does His will, He hears him" (John 9:31 NASB). *There's the key.* We must deal with our sin *first*. We must repent of it, get it out of our heart and out of our life. And the only way to get it out is to come to the Lord and ask for His forgiveness. The Bible says, "If we confess our sins, He is faithful and just to forgive us *our* sins, and to cleanse us from all unrighteousness" (1 John 1:9 AKJV). And He not only forgives, but He forgets our sins too!

Another serious hinderance to prayer is found and clearly explained in Mark 11:25. Its about not forgiving. An unforgiving spirit is one of the most common hinderances to prayer. Prayer is answered on the basis that our sins are forgiven. However, God cannot deal with us on a basis of forgiveness while we are still harboring ill will against those who have wronged us. Anyone who is nursing a grudge against another has closed the ear of God against his own petition. Now just imagine if you will how many people are crying to God in prayer for the conversion of a husband, wife, children, friends, and wondering why it is that their prayer is not answered. The whole secret to their problem is some grudge that they may have in their hearts against someone who has injured them. We *must* learn to forgive as our heavenly Father has forgiven us.

A rebellious person may want to pray, but he may not want to "hear" or "abide." God will speak to the rebellious heart to repent of sin, but if no change occurs, God will not force His will, and God will not speak on other subjects. Remember, rebellion blocks God's penetrating voice (see John 9:31) and as Jesus explained when He said, "I am the vine and you are the branches," and *because of their unbelief,* they were "broken off" (see Romans 11:20). "Witness the simultaneous balance of the kindness and severity of our God. Severity is directed at the fallen *branches withering without faith*. Yet kindness is directed at you. So live in the kindness of God or else prepare to be cut off yourselves. If those branches that have been cut off from the tree do not stay in unbelief, then God will carefully graft them back onto the tree because He has the power to do that" (see Rom. 11:22-23 VOICE). Remember, that prayer, coupled with loving obedience and genuine repentance, is the answer to all ends and blessings.

Therefore, wanting to be obedient to our Lord and His Word, we also need be *careful* to whom we pray. Why? Because praying to someone other than God is idolatry! Jesus has made it both clear and evident to whom we pray. (See Matthew 6:5-15). Jesus said we are to pray to the Father. Saying the Rosary and praying to Mary is praying to someone other than God, and the Bible tells us it's not Mary who is our mediator. Scripture declares it is Jesus Christ the righteous, "He Himself is the propitiation for our sins." Our only advocate and mediator between God and man is Jesus Christ. Not Mary or any other saint. "And so He is able, now and always, to save those who come to God through Him, because He lives forever to plead with God for them" (Heb. 7:25 GNT). Christ is the door to heaven, and Jesus said, "I am the door; if anyone enters through Me, he shall be saved" (John 10:9 NASB). Jesus said, "I am the Light of the world; he who follows Me, will not remain in darkness, but will have the Light of life" (John 8:12 NASB). Scripture tells us it is "Christ Jesus, who is our hope" (1 Tim. 1:1 NASB). Praying to Mary was devised by man and religion and runs contrary to *all* biblical instructions. Our Lord also tells us, "And when you are praying, do not use meaningless repetition, as the Gentiles do, for they suppose that they will be heard for their many words. Therefore, do not be like them; for your Father knows what you need, before you ask Him" (Matt. 6:7-8 NASB).

Jesus said, "Whatever you ask in My name, that will I do" (John 14:13-14 NASB). Jesus said, "Come to me, all who labor and are heavy-laden, and I will give you rest" (Matt. 11:28 ESV). Jesus said, "I am the way, and the truth, and the Life; no one comes to the Father but *through me*" (John 14:6 NASB). "There is salvation in no one else; for there is no other name under heaven that has been given among men, by which we must be saved" (Acts 4:12 NASB).

The Bible does *not* accord to Mary or any other person or "saint" any attributes of deity, nor a single statement or verse urging us to pray to them. If Jesus wanted people to pray to His earthly mother, He would have said so. The Bible does not accord Mary as the great mediator or that salvation is to be had through her. And the Bible does not describe Mary as a person to be worshiped or to be called the Mother of God.

To imply that Mary was the "mother of God" would imply that she existed before God. God has never accepted Mary as His partner in dispensing His favors or as His equal; and He has never shared His honor or glory with her. The Bible says, "I am the Lord, that is My name; I will not give My glory to another, nor My praise to graven images" (Isa. 42:8 NASB).

We are to pray to our Creator only! Mary was just a creature of God like all other human beings. She was the mother of the natural body [Jesus] that God incarnated. To worship or pray to a creature is contrary to God's will. God's Holy Word says, "Who exchanged the truth of God for the lie, and worshiped and served the creature rather than the Creator, who is blessed forever" (Rom. 1:25 NKJV). Why have recourse to Mary or any other "saint," when an all-sufficient, all powerful, all loving Savior promises to supply our needs through Christ, God's *chosen one*, and the only mediator between God and man? As Scripture states, "Show me Your ways, O Lord; Teach me Your paths. Lead me in Your truth and teach me, for You *are* the God of my salvation, on *You* I wait all day" (Ps. 25:4-5 NKJV).

Our prayers should *always* be in accordance with God's will, and prayer is not only asking, but it is also *listening* to Him. Pray before studying the Bible and you will discover wisdom and understanding and a fellowship with our Lord. God urges us to bring our concerns to Him. Prayer is a lifeline to our God. One of the best ways to pray to God is to open our Bible and pray Scripture back to Him, claiming His promises. And no matter how dark or how depressing and hopeless a situation might be, never stop praying to Him. If we are to count on prayer during difficult times, then we should be people of prayer *before* crisis hits.

However, we must always remember that whatever God's decision, God causes all things to work for His purpose, and as Scripture says, to work out together for the *good* to those who love God, to those who are called according to His purpose (see Romans 8:28). An illness and death of a person doesn't necessarily mean that God didn't answer prayers. It may mean the very opposite and that prayers were answered for God to call him or her home. As humans we sometimes tend to be selfish and want to "hold back" a person from ever leaving this life, when God who knows better, has something supremely and infinitely better that's prepared for him or her. I would bet that every person God calls home to his Kingdom was mightily pleased!! God in His infinite wisdom and love for His children truly knows what's best for us. He knows what He's doing and sometimes His denials or delays are truly a benediction. We are blessed by what He grants and blessed by what He denies.

How doubt and disregard for God's instruction in the Bible and unbelief of men has also "limited" the power of God to work through prayer! Make no mistake about it. It virtually kills the power of all prayers. "For let not that man think that he shall receive any thing of the Lord" (James 1:7 KJV). Why? "Because without faith it is impossible to please Him, for he who comes to God *must believe* that He is, and that He is a rewarder of those who diligently seek Him" (Heb. 11:6 NKJV).

God's eternal Word also indicates there are other reasons why some prayers are not answered. Example: Asking for the wrong reasons (James 4:3), disobedience (1 John 3:22), asking out of the will of God (1 John 5:14). According to 1 Peter 3:7, unanswered or unfruitful prayer can even stem from insensitivity in a marriage relationship. Peter stated that a husband's prayers are "hindered" if he isn't loving his wife as he should.

For these reasons, God wants us to understand that *obedience to God counts tremendously* in the realm of prayer. Therefore, listen to Him, let Him be your guide, and strength and help will come to you. God is evermore ready to listen than you to ask! But remember, God's listening to your voice depends upon *your listening to His* voice. God says "He who turns away his ear from listening to the law, even his prayer is an abomination" (Prov. 28:9 NASB).

Therefore, listen to His words. "Be anxious for nothing, but in everything by prayer and supplication, with thanksgiving, let your requests be made known to God; and the peace of God, which surpasses all understanding, will guard your hearts and minds through Christ Jesus" (Phi. 4:6-7 NKJV). A life *yielding* to the glory of God is the "condition" for the prayers that our Lord can answer.

CHAPTER 34

According to Our Lord,
Is There Forgiveness of Sin
to All Who Repent? Yes.

I t was also written that this message would be proclaimed in the
authority of His name to all the nations, beginning in Jerusalem,
"There is forgiveness of sins for all who repent" (Luke 24:47 NLT).
"The Son of Man has authority on earth to forgive sins" (Luke 5:24 ESV).
"The times of ignorance God overlooked, but now He commands all
people everywhere to repent, because He has fixed a day on which He
will judge the world in righteousness by a man whom He has appointed,
[Christ Jesus] and of this He has given assurance to all by raising Him
from the dead" (Acts 17:30-31 ESV). "Repent, and each of you be
baptized in the name of Jesus Christ for the forgiveness of your sins;
and you will receive the gift of the Holy Spirit. For this promise is for
you and your children and for all who are far off, as many as the Lord
our God will call to Himself" (Acts 2:38-39, NASB). "Repent therefore
and be converted, that your sins may be blotted out" (Acts 3:19 NKJV).

The gift of the Holy Spirit and the promise that our sins may be
blotted out does not come upon those accepting Jesus Christ and
making a profession of faith, yet shows no difference in the their attitude
and behavior. Many who name the name of Christ and profess to be

Christians have failed to "depart from their iniquity [Lawlessness]" (2 Tim. 2:19). They are false converts who have "asked Jesus into their hearts," yet they remain unconverted because they have never truly repented. We cannot be "converted" *unless* we repent. That is why Jesus *commanded* that repentance, and not penance be preached to all nations.

Comment: Do you know that we have all been found guilty of sin by our Holy God and therefore sentenced to eternal punishment? If we are to escape this eternal punishment and be eternally saved, we must receive God's mercy. Mercy in this respect is God withholding from us the penalty we deserve. But God does not bestow His mercy on people *without condition*, even though salvation is free, without cost, and cannot be earned. The condition upon which God grants mercy is *repentance*, not penance.

Repentance is so important it's mentioned over sixty times in the New Testament. God commands repentance, and says, "Repent or perish!" Repentance qualifies a man for salvation, but it takes faith and belief in Christ to accept it. True repentance is always coupled with faith. To clarify, repentance involves not only sorrow for sin, but *turning away* from wrongdoing and a change to do right. A repentance that does not produce a change in character and conduct is a mere sham that shouldn't fool anyone. "For the kind of sorrow God wants makes people change their hearts and lives. This leads to salvation" (2 Corin. 7:10 NCV). Finally, repentance results in a deep appreciation and loyalty to Christ and God's will. As Scripture says, "The old life is gone; a new life has begun!" (2 Cor. 5:17 NLT). "Truly, truly, I say to you, unless one is born again [of the Spirit and believes], he cannot see the Kingdom of God" (John 3:3 NASB).

God loves us even if we are living in sin. His love has made a way for us to be saved (see John 3:16). God will carry out His judgment on sin, and if this justice were meted out to man, man would be instantly cast into eternal punishment. However, God is not willing that any should perish and sent His Son, Jesus, to take the penalty of our sins that we may live.

The Bible says: "Behold then the kindness and severity of God" (Rom. 11:22 NASB). The kindness of God desires to save man but His judgment demands justice. In other words, salvation is a life-and-death choice. Scripture says "But unless you repent, you will all likewise perish" (Luke 13:3 NASB). Therefore, "Bear fruits in keeping with repentance" (see Matt. 3:8 ESV; Luke 3:8 ESV). Remember, there is one thing God's love can never do for mankind. God can never forgive an unrepentant sinner and person who forever rejects His Son, Jesus.

Yes, Scripture says there is forgiveness of sins to *all* who repent. However, Scripture also warns, "Those who have been pulled out of the cesspool of worldly desires through the knowledge of our Lord and Savior Jesus Christ, the Anointed One, yet have found themselves mired in it again are worse off than they were before. They would have been better off never knowing the way of righteousness than to have known it and then abandoned the sacred commandment they had previously received" (2 Peter 2:20-21 VOICE). "None of the righteous things that person has done will be remembered. Because of the unfaithfulness they are guilty of and because of the sins they have committed, they will die" (Exek.18:24 NIV). "But if a wicked man turns from all his sins he has committed, keeps all My statutes, and does what is lawful and right, he shall surely live; he shall not die. None of the transgressions which he has committed shall be remembered against him; because of the righteousness which he has done, he shall live" (Ezek. 18:21-22 NKJV).

In view of all this, make *every effort* to respond to God's promises. He says in Scripture, "So don't lose a minute in building on what you've been given, complementing your basic faith with good character, spiritual understanding, alert discipline, passionate patience, reverent wonder, warm friendliness, and generous love, each dimension fitting into and developing the others. With these qualities active and growing in your lives, no day will pass without its reward as you mature in your experience of our Master Jesus. Without these qualities you can't see what's right before you, oblivious that your old sinful life has been wiped off the books" (2 Peter 1:5-9 MSG).

"So, friends, confirm God's invitation to you, His choice of you. Don't put it off; do it now. Do this, and you'll have your life on a firm footing, the streets paved and the way wide open into the eternal kingdom of our Master and Savior, Jesus Christ" (2 Peter 1:10 MSG). "Blessed are those who hear the Word of God, and observe it" (Luke 11:28 NASB). Remember, "there is forgiveness of sins for all who repent" (Luke 24:47 NLT).

While repentance is necessary for God's forgiveness of sin, the concept of confession of sin to a priest is nowhere taught in Scripture. None of the apostles ever forgave a person's sin. They always directed their listeners to Jesus Christ and Him *alone*. We can approach our Lord's throne directly (Hebrews 4:16), and in prayer and petition seek His forgiveness. A sinner can receive forgiveness *directly* from God through faith. It is not necessary nor a requirement of God to avail ourselves to a priest's mediation for forgiveness. The Scriptures are very clear.

No priest or minister is needed to mediate between God and man, "For there is one God, *and* one mediator also between God and men, *the* man Christ Jesus" (1 Tim. 2:5 NASB). "In *Him* [alone], we have redemption through His blood, the forgiveness of sins, according to the riches of His grace" (Eph. 1:7 NASB). "Therefore let it be know to you, brethren, that through *Him* [Christ], forgiveness of sins is proclaimed to you" (Acts 13:38 NASB). The *only* One who can forgive sin is the One who is sinless. "For He made Him who knew no sin to be sin on our behalf, that we might become the righteousness of God in Him" (2 Corin. 5:21 NASB).

According to our Lord there *is* forgiveness of sins for **all** who repent, and abiding by *His* Word of repentance and baptism He promises this; "You **will** receive the gift of the Holy Spirit." However, in abiding by

His Word we must always remember His message; That there is only one person who can forgive your sin. There is only one person who paid for your sin. There is only one person who is your Mediator, and there is only one person who can give you eternal life. That person is Jesus Christ. He said "*I am the way*, the truth and the life, no one comes to the Father but through Me" (John 14:6 NASB). There is no other way. And "Of *Him*, all the prophets bear witness that through *His name*, everyone who believes in *Him*, receives forgiveness of sins" (Acts 10:43 NASB).

Your final destination whether it be Heaven or Hell will depend on who's side your on, who you trust and believe, the words of man and his religion, or the words of our Lord and Savior Jesus Christ and the Holy Bible. Jesus declared; "Everyone on the side of truth listens to Me" (John 18:37 NIV). Christ and *His* words of instruction should therefore be your primary guidance and final authority pertaining to life, God and eternal salvation, as truly, neither man nor religion nor any government can ever save you. "We must obey God rather than men" (Acts 5:29). "Your faith should not rest on the wisdom of men, but on the Power of God" (1 Corin. 2:5 NASB).

Parts 5 and 6

Scriptural Summary Points to Remember

- Through knowledge of Him, God has granted us everything pertaining to life.

- According to God's great mercy, those born again to a living hope through Christ, are to obtain an inheritance which is imperishable and undefiled, and will not fade away, and reserved in heaven for them, who are protected by the power of God through faith for a salvation to be revealed.

- These things I have written to you [in the Bible] who *believe* in the name of the Son of God, so that you may *know* [while still alive] that you have eternal life.

- All unrighteousness and unbelief is sin and a rebellious act against God.

- Rebellion blocks God's penetrating voice.

- The unpardonable sin is an unrepentant heart and *rejection* of our Lord Jesus Christ.

- Sin separates us from God so that He does not hear us. We are broken off for our unbelief.

- For the wages of sin is death, but the free gift of God is eternal life in Christ Jesus our Lord.

- There is forgiveness of sins for all who repent. Repent, therefore, and be converted, that your sins may be blotted out.

- Unless you repent, you will all likewise perish.

- We are commanded to pray because of its all-prevailing power for the child of God (the believer).

- If you want prayer to be powerful, you need to become a child of God. In order to be a child of God, you must receive and believe in the Lord Jesus as your personal Savior.

- We need be careful to *whom* we pray because we have an all-sufficient, all powerful, all loving Savior who promises to supply our needs through Christ, God's chosen one, and the *only* mediator between God and man.

- Obedience to God counts *tremendously* in the realm of prayer and eternal salvation.

- Christ was God's witness and *His* testimony *must* be accepted for prayer to prevail. God Himself said, "This is My Son, My chosen one, Listen to Him."

PART 7

False Religions, Varied Teachings, and the Consequence of Unbelief

Has God Forewarned Mankind about False Religions and Teachers? What Book, Therefore, Has God Commanded We Read and Study?

"For the time will come when they will not endure sound doctrine; but wanting to have their ears tickled, they will accumulate for themselves teachers in accordance to their own desires, and will turn away their ears from the truth, and will turn aside to myths" (2 Tim. 4:3-4 NASB). "But in vain do they worship me, teaching as doctrines the precepts of men. Neglecting the commandments of God, you hold to the tradition of men" (Mark 7:7-8 NASB).

"You nicely set aside the commandment of God in order to keep your [religious] tradition, *thus* invalidating the Word of God by your tradition . . . as you do many things such as that" (Mark 7:9, 13 NASB). "Wanting to be teachers of the law, even though they do not understand either what they are saying or the matters about which they make confident assertions" (1 Tim. 1:7 NASB). "Woe to you, teachers of the law . . . you hypocrites! You shut the door of the kingdom of heaven in people's faces. You yourselves do not enter, nor will you let those enter who are trying to" (Matt. 23:13 NIV). "Holding to a form of godliness, although they have denied its power; Avoid such men as these . . . always learning and never able to come to the knowledge of the truth" (2 Tim.

3:5, 7 NASB). "For *many* will come in My name . . . and will mislead many" (Matt. 24:5 NASB).

Comment: Recognizing false teachings! Today tracts, magazines, books, CDs, radio, and television are flooding the world, many with false and misleading teachings. Great care must be taken to choose our reading material or what we listen to wisely. If we don't read and study the Bible as God instructed us and don't know Scripture well enough to discern what is truth and what is false, and then we open our minds to teachings of religions and cults not fully based on the gospel of Christ and the word of God in Scripture, then Satan will have an easy chance of dangerously misleading us away from God's truth and ultimately from eternal life in heaven.

According to Scripture, the only absolute head of the true church is Jesus Christ, and the true church is not identified with any one specific organization but with all the redeemed people of God. "See to it that no one takes you captive through philosophy and empty deception, according to the traditions of men; according to the elementary principles of the world, rather than according to Christ" (Col. 2:8 NASB). "Don't be deceived!! Every word of God is tested" (Prov. 30:5 NASB). "Do not add to His words or He will reprove you, and you will be proved a liar (Prov. 30:6 ESV). "Do not go beyond what is written" (1 Corin. 4:6 NIV).

Maybe you are thinking, "Well, surely there are some ministers who would dare to deliberately twist God's Word and deceive many people, but the ministers I know are good sincere and honest men." And undoubtedly there are *many* very good and sincere men in the ministry. But it's possible to be sincere and yet be very much deceived. It is entirely possible to be sincerely wrong! Ask yourself, why do we have so many thousands of different religions and denominations in the world today? It's like a vast religious supermarket. Whatever one's likes or approach to religion is, there's something out there.

In evangelical churches today, regardless of how positive and good their messages may sound, without the foundation of Bible teaching, and teaching the *unadulterated* word of God, those churches are committing spiritual adultery. That is what apostasy is all about: Forsaking the true meaning and message of Biblical doctrine, or choosing which doctrines to believe and which to discard.

Yet Scripture *very clearly* states that *any* deviation from God's teachings to embrace other doctrines will cause one to depart from the faith and forfeit union with God. Scripture affirms, "Whosoever transgresseth, and abideth not in the doctrine of Christ, hath not God" (2 John 9 KJ21). Christ said, "If you abide in My Word, *then*, you are truly My disciples, and you will know the truth, and the truth [regarding salvation] will set you free" (John 8:31-32 AMP).

This means, according to Scripture, to *really* know the truth, as God would want you to know it, we must abide in *His* Word, not the word and doctrines of man and religion, but *Christ's Word*. Scripture says, "Let the word of Christ richly dwell within you" (Col. 3:16 NASB). Doing this we comply with Scripture. Remember that rebellion to God's Word and the doctrine of Christ blocks God's penetrating voice! Therefore, according to God's word in the Bible, no religion and no man can claim to "represent God" and know the "truth" as God would want him to know it, if such person or religion is so progressive in their thinking they deviate from the teachings of Christ. For Scripture *clearly* warns us; "Everyone who does **not** continue to teach what Christ taught does not have God. The person who continues to teach what Christ taught, has both the Father and the Son" (2 John 9 GW).

Because of the demonic influence the world is under, many religions today are endeavoring to keep people out of God's kingdom by distorting, suppressing, and contradicting our Lord's Word in the Gospel, and thereby perverting God's way of salvation. Example: By preaching to people that because "God is love, God will not punish His people," and a "good" God would never condemn anyone to hell," they lead people to be content with themselves and to see no need for repentance and salvation, thereby shutting tight the gracious door God has provided. By believing this lie, they are oblivious to the fate that awaits them. This teaching not only contradicts numerous direct statements of Christ in the Bible, which say evil men will be cast into eternal punishment forever, but it also *distorts* the concept of love and its relationship to the other attributes of God. Love may have to punish, and the attribute of love does not operate in God apart from His other attributes, particularly the attribute of holiness and His requirement of conforming to absolute righteousness and justice. Just as we expect the courts to render justice and punishment, so will our Lord as He said.

Similarly, when people are told through their religion that they can "work their way" into God's kingdom by performing certain "good deeds," or by participating in some prescribed religious ritual, they are likewise deceived and left in their lost condition. The true disciples of Christ will abide by *Christ's Word* and proclaim the gospel that Christ Himself preached. Remember, sin is so very serious and repulsive in the eyes of God that Christ suffered and died for sin, in order for man to be saved. He does not want anyone to go into eternal punishment. But unless and until we believe, repent, and surrender our lives to Jesus Christ, we are headed for eternal damnation. Throughout Scripture, God gives warning that He will exact punishment and pour out His wrath on Judgment Day because of unrepentant sin and unbelief.

With so many different religions worldwide, it is absolutely imperative that we properly identify God's true church for fellowship and worship from those that are false and misleading. Why? Because when judgment day comes, one cannot claim "ignorance" of God's laws and being "misled" by a false religion, and then ask God for a "pass" into heaven. That will not happen. God's instructions for salvation are very simple and very clear. As adults, we are each responsible for our own eternal destiny, and that destiny will be determined by our actions and our temporary life here on earth.

Jesus has forewarned us in Matthew 24:11 that many false prophets (religions) will rise up and deceive many. Today, the voices of those who claim to represent God are being raised everywhere. So how can you know for certain who does and does not really represent Him? In other words, how can you discern the true church of God? The answer: *A thorough knowledge of your Bible* is the best insurance you can have against being led astray into doctrinal error. This is why God *commands us* to *read* His book, to *study* His book, to *meditate* on His book, to *abide* in His words. Why? Because God knows you will be alert to the truth and better equipped to detect and recognize perverse teachings. The Bible says of God's words; "There is nothing crooked or perverted in them" (Prov. 8:8 NASB). "They are all straightforward to him who understands, and right to those who find knowledge" (Prov. 8:9 NASB).

Know that God's true church is one that must *genuinely* represent the God of the Bible and fully accept the Bible for what it claims itself to be, the inerrant Word of God. It must preach the unadulterated Word of God and do it in its entirety. The true church will not bend to the pressures and influence of the world or its culture and then re-create different religious doctrines contrary to the gospel. Rather, the central mission of the true church is to uphold and proclaim the gospel of Christ to the world. Equally important, and in keeping with Scripture, the true church must absolutely side with and be supportive of Israel.

The Lord has made it abundantly clear the fate of **all** people and **all** nations who think otherwise. Thus declares the Lord... "And it will come about in that day that I will set about to destroy all the nations that come against Jerusalem" (Zech. 12:9 NASB). "Now this will be the plague with which the Lord will strike all the peoples who have gone to war against Jerusalem; their flesh will rot while they stand on their feet, and their eyes will rot in their sockets, and their tongue will rot in their mouth. And it will come about in that day that a great panic from the Lord will fall on them" (Zech. 14:12-13 NASB).

Men are at liberty to reject Jesus Christ and the Bible as the Word of God if they so choose. They are free to deny Him. They are free to challenge and discredit Him. But they are not at liberty to change and alter the essential God-given message in the Bible. Today there are churches that wrongly attempt to "read into Scripture" some "new hidden meanings" that are diametrically opposed to the very words of Christ. Interpreters who do this end up doing *exactly* what God sternly warns them *not to do*, that is, taking away or adding to the very words of Scripture. (See Rev. 22:18-19.) When the plain sense of Scripture makes common sense, seek no other sense. Churches are to draw God's truth *from* Scripture, not superimpose their own pre-conceived ideas onto it.

The true Christian church will not discredit, distort, or delete any part of Scripture or the gospel of Christ in the Bible. Whoever criticizes, challenges, or questions the Bible's authority or distorts, adds, or subtracts from the Word of God is ultimately undermining the divine authority of our Lord and putting man the creature in place of God the Creator. Remember, Scripture says, "Every Word of God is tested, flawless, and proves true" (see Prov. 30:5 NASB, NIV, NLT). And to make sure that we do not overlook the importance of God's truthfulness, three times the Scripture affirms that God cannot lie (see Heb. 6:18 KJV, Titus 1:2, KJV, Num. 23:19 KJV).

The Bible declares, "The entirety of thy Word *is* truth, and every one of your righteous judgments endures forever" (Ps. 119:160 NKJV). Nations have rejected it, tyrants have tried to stamp it out, and some religions have tried to distort it, but the evidence for the Bible's reliability is overwhelming, and as Scripture says, "Heaven and earth shall pass away but my words shall not pass away" (Matt. 24:35 KJV). Almighty God has given strong evidence that we can trust His Word. He *emphasized it*, and His message was made to reassure us of that fact. Don't allow people or religion to convince you otherwise. They cannot save you!

God has gone to great lengths over many generations of time, through Noah, Abraham, Moses, and so many other prophets, including through the apostles, through His Son Jesus, through thousands of ancient manuscripts, and to this day through the Bible, to show that He loves us, cares for us, and wants us to be with Him. Truly, God has given more than ample and credible evidence of His love and life-saving Word. For thousands of years He has "pleaded" that we pay attention to *Him*, listen to *Him*, abide in *Him*, and acquire wisdom and understanding of *His* Word, because it is *life* to those who believe.

The Word of God is your *true source* of wisdom and God will give you this wisdom. "But [you must] grow in the grace and in the knowledge of our Lord and Savior Jesus Christ" (2 Peter 3:18 NASB). "Plant your roots in Christ and let *Him* be the foundation for your life" (Col. 2:7 CEV). Jesus said, "If you abide in *My Word* . . . then, you will know the truth and the truth will set you free" (John 8:31-32 AMP).

CHAPTER 36

What Has God Said about Church Teachings that Are Varied and Different?

Warning: "Do not be carried away by varied and strange teachings" (Heb. 13:9 NASB). "For such men are false apostles, deceitful workers, disguising themselves as apostles of Christ. And no wonder, for even Satan disguises himself as an angel of light. Therefore it is not surprising if his servants also disguise themselves as servants of righteousness, whose end will be according to their deeds" (2 Cor. 11:13-15 NASB).

"Now I urge you, brethren, keep your eye on those who cause dissensions and hindrances *contrary* to the teachings which you learned, and turn away from them" (Rom. 16:17 NASB). "These kinds of people are not truly serving our Lord Jesus the Anointed; they have devoted their lives to satisfying their own appetites. With smooth talking and a *well-rehearsed* blessing, they lead a lot of unsuspecting people down the wrong path." (Rom. 16:18 VOICE). Rather, listen to our Lord. He tells us, "We have the Prophetic Word made *more sure*, to which you do well to pay attention" (2 Peter 1:19 NASB).

Again, Scripture warns: "If anyone advocates a 'different doctrine,' and does not agree with the sound Words of our Lord Jesus Christ, and with the doctrine conforming to godliness, he is conceited *and* understands nothing; but he has a morbid interest in controversial questions and disputes about words, out of which arise envy, strife, abusive language, evil suspicions, . . . men of depraved mind and depraved of the truth, who suppose that godliness is a means of gain" (1 Tim. 6:3-5 NASB). "Whoever transgresses and does not abide in the doctrine of Christ, does not have God. He who abides in the doctrine of Christ has both the Father and the Son" (2 John 9 NKJV). "Jesus Christ is the same yesterday, and today, and for ever" (Heb. 13:8 KJV). Therefore His teachings do *not* change ever with time.

Comment: If we allow a love for self and the culture of the world to blind our eyes to the will of God, we will develop a resistance to God's will and grieve the Spirit of God. Then Satan comes in as an "angel of light" and we listen to him, because it "appeals" to our carnal mind. Little by little we accept a broader, easier way, thinking all is okay. To think we are right when we are wrong is deception, and Satan is the big player and deceiver in all this.

Understand that there's a powerful demonic influence affecting the world today. Look at the Supreme Court rulings in America declaring of all things that prayer, Bible reading and posting the Ten Commandments in public schools to be unconstitutional, thereby effectively prohibiting the teaching of righteous and moral values! With the Ten Commandments kept out of all public schools during our children's most important and formative years, it should be no surprise that detrimental results have arisen throughout society. This is clearly seen in increasing family breakdown, sexual promiscuity, violence, pornography, abortion to date of childbirth in New York, rising drug and alcohol addiction, crime and other evils. Truly, a systematic effort is at work in America and other Western countries to expel God and His commandments from public and private life, striking at the very foundation of our culture.

America has publicly abandoned the Bible as the moral anchor of our society and education so it should surprise no one that, after decades of teaching our children that there are no absolute rights or wrongs, we face an appalling breakdown in public morality and rising levels of crime, corruption and growing use of mind altering substances such as narcotics and hallucinogens. Satan through religion and every other means is effectively steering people away from God's truth and thereby affecting our culture. We now have more false religions than ever before. This is not a time to go shopping around and exploring for different religions and doctrine. Truly, if there was ever a time for us to be unequivocal about the truth then this is it! The big buzzword being spoken today is tolerance. Oh we need more tolerance. I want to be only as tolerant as God is, but God is very intolerant of what is not true!

Just look at international events! Evil has progressed in all nations. Satan's avowed purpose is to thwart the plan of God in every area and by every way possible. Satan knows the best way to deceive many people is to *conceal his true intentions,* disguise himself as an angel of light, and deceive through religion. And Satan has a rage for God's people and particularly the Jews.

Throughout the world, but particularly with Christians and Jews, Satan is trying to get God's people to follow a "counterfeit plan" instead of doing the will of God. He is most cunning and knows the best way in the world to deceive people is to cloak a message in religious language and declare that it conveys some new meaning from God. As Scripture tells us, "In whose case the god of this world has blinded the minds of the unbelievers, that they might not see the light of the gospel of the glory of Christ" (2 Cor. 4:4 NASB). Understand that not every religion in the world nor every building that has a cross on it proclaims the *true gospel* and sound words of our Lord Jesus Christ.

Know Scripture well enough to identify and detect what is true and what is false. When we know the unshakable truth, the factual evidence in Scripture, and we are presented with that which is false, we will *instinctively* recognize it. Being capable of measuring philosophies or theologies or opinions or religious sermons or church doctrines by the Word of God is so *critically important*, in determining truth or falsehood in a fallen world of deception and demonic influence. Your eternal destination is at stake! Know whom you are trusting for your eternity!

"You therefore, beloved, knowing this *beforehand*, be on your guard so that you are not carried away by the error of unprincipled men and fall . . . but grow in the grace and knowledge of our Lord and Savior Jesus Christ" (2 Peter 3:17-18 NASB). For neither man nor religion can save you. Scripture clearly warns us "Fools die for lack of understanding" (Prov. 10:21 NASB). " . . . but through *knowledge* the righteous will be delivered" (Prov. 11:9 NASB). And for over two thousand years our Lord Jesus has been pleading through the Scriptures to "come to Me" and "learn from Me, for I am gentle and humble in heart, and you will find rest for your souls" (Matt. 11:28-29 NASB). Listen to Him!

Don't listen to the voice of Satan. He is able to take control of Christians thinking anytime they begin believing him. Jesus stressed and forewarned us of Satan's violence and deceit. "He was a murderer from the beginning. He has always hated the truth, because there is no truth in him. When he lies, it is consistent with his character; for he is a liar and the father of lies" (John 8:44 NLT). Satan's most common means for capturing believers is to gain control over their minds by so deceiving them that they no longer think like believers. We need to recognize that when Satan induces doubt and disbelief of God's truth and message in a person, if they believe that first lie it won't be just a mistake but an entry point for Satan. When they yield at one point the danger will increase dramatically for them. Satan never lets people off with an isolated case of deception. Oh no, he will press on and on with one point after another until he gains control of their thinking. Believing Satan is a very deadly slippery slope. The Bible states; "So humble yourselves before God. Resist the devil, and he will flee from you" (James 4:7 NLT).

God knows Satan's evil intentions, and for *this* reason, God has *clearly* forewarned us and provided us *much guidance* to protect us from deception and false religions. Over and over God commands: "Turn to My reproof, Behold, I will pour out My Spirit on you; I will make My Words known to you" (Prov. 1:23 NASB). Read *carefully* some of our Lord's specific instructions in Proverbs 2:1-12, Proverbs 7:1-5, Proverbs 8:32-36, and Proverbs 24:13-14. Have you taken the time to read it? If not, stop! Please, stop. Look them up in your Bible. Don't proceed until you have read it. Its too important. God goes to great lengths emphasizing a point and driving a message for the benefit of *your* security. As the Bible states in Proverbs 8:33-34 NASB, heed the instruction and be wise. Do not neglect it!

True Christians who study and meditate on His words as God instructed are alert in truth, and therefore better equipped to detect and recognize perverse teachings. Our Lord knows the closer we walk with *Him*, the clearer we see *His* guidance! How blessed, thankful, and grateful we should be for our Lord's loving guidance and wisdom. Listen what clear and commanding statements God has put in the divine record the Bible to provide us wisdom, guidance and direction for truth. It reads; "My son, do not forget *My* teachings, but let your heart keep *My* commandments; For length of days and years of life and peace they will add to you. Do not let kindness and truth leave you; Bind them around your neck, Write them on the tablet of your heart. So you will find favor and good repute in the sight of God and man. Trust in the Lord with all your heart and do not lean on your own understanding. In all your ways acknowledge Him, and He will make your paths straight. Do not be wise in your own eyes; Fear the Lord and turn away from evil. It will be healing to your body and refreshment to your bones. Honor the Lord from your wealth and from the first of all your produce; So your barns will be filled with plenty and your vats will overflow with new wine. My son, do not reject the discipline of the Lord or loathe His reproof, For whom the Lord loves He reproves, even as a father corrects the son in whom he delights. How blessed is the man who finds wisdom and the man who gains understanding. For her profit is better than the profit of silver and her gain better than fine gold" (Proverbs 3:1-14 NASB).

As Scripture instructs for our own benefit; we are to turn to His wisdom, walk in His ways, keep His statutes, His commandments, His testimonies, and specifically abide and *saturate ourselves* in the teachings of Christ, in order to distinguish the voice of God from the voice of Satan! God instructs us to read and study *His* book to recognize and turn away from perversions of Scripture and to stand fast in defense of the faith. Question: Are you risking your eternal life by believing in varied and different teachings, in the doctrines of man and religion *rather* than the true gospel of Christ and the Bible?

CHAPTER 37

According to God, How Many Bodies of Believers and Faiths Should There Be?

T he Bible *clearly* states: "There is one body [of believers] and one spirit, just as you were called to one hope when called [to salvation], one Lord, one faith, one baptism, and one God and Father of us all" (Eph. 4:4-6 AMP). Again, that is *one* body of believers, *one* faith, and *one* God! God confirms this message through Christ His Son when He says, "I will build My church" (Matt. 16:18 NASB). Whose church? Christ's church. Jesus did not say "churches"; He said "church." The word *church* is singular. Christ only built up one true church, and one body of believers. According to the Bible, "He is also head of the body, the church" (Col. 1:18 NASB). "Christ also loved the church and gave Himself up [died] for her" (Eph. 5:25 NASB). Christ has only one church " . . . which He purchased with His own blood" (Acts 20:28 NASB).

If we expect to be saved, we must be in the Lord's body of believers, His one true church, and not in any of the man-made denominational churches having *different and varied* teachings. According to Scripture, there is only one body of believers and one faith, and the only absolute head of the one true church is Jesus Christ. The one true church is not identified with any specific organization but with all redeemed people of God. In other words, the *only* true church is made up of individuals who have fully accepted Jesus Christ as their Lord and Savior, and abide in *His* teachings and message.

Yet as of 2014, it is estimated that there are 4,200 *different* religions in the world, of which Christianity is one. According to the World Christian Encyclopedia (2nd edition, 2001), world Christianity consists of six major cultural blocs, divided into 300 major ecclesiastical traditions, composed of over 33,000 "distinct" Christian denominations in 238 countries, these denominations themselves being composed of over 3,400,000 worship centers, churches, or congregations" (volume 1, page 16, Table 1-5). While there are also many different and distinct religions worldwide other than Christianity, the number of different forms of god's believed in and worshipped is beyond count. Scripture tells us that in the end times, many people will flock to counterfeit forms of Christianity, cults and religions that perverts and twists the faith to suit the desires and wishes of their own beliefs.

Certainly, there are many God-fearing churches that are preaching the one true gospel of Christ as Scripture instructs. However, with multiple thousands of different religions, God has warned us not to be deceived by a tangled web of world religions and cults that lure millions of people into "false" hopes, that teach "man-made doctrines" and beliefs. Examine the source of their authority. Do they deny the biblical way of salvation and preach another gospel? False preachers and religions continued all down through the centuries to deceive the comparatively uneducated masses who thirst for a relationship with their Creator.

Christianity's source of authority is Jesus Christ as revealed in the Bible. The Bible is our Lord's instruction and rule of law for Christian faith, belief, and salvation. False religions and cults will not allow the Holy Bible to be the final source of authority for everything.

The popular evangelist message of our time actually lures people into deception. It promises their followers a wonderful plan for everyone's life. It obliterates the work of the cross. Its subject is the love of God, but gives no mention of God's wrath. It is full of love and understanding, but teaches no word of a holy God who hates sin. There is tolerance of every conceivable sin, just as long as you say you love God, or as long as you are religious. There is no teaching of repentance, no warning of judgement, no expectation of remorse, and no reason for deep sorrow over sin. Oh its a message of an easy salvation, often accompanied by false promises of health, happiness and material blessing. This however is *not* the gospel according to Jesus.

Jesus warned us not to be misled. When the disciples asked Jesus about the signs of His coming and the end of the age, the very first thing Jesus did was to give a warning, "See to it that no one misleads you, for many will come in My name" (Matt. 24:4-5, NASB). Six verses later Jesus again repeats the warning about deception when He says "And many false prophets will arise, and will mislead many" (Matt. 24:11 NASB). Today Satan is bringing great deception to the world to deceive as many people as he can in order to keep them out of God's kingdom. Religious deception is now widespread and basically unrecognized.

Here's the issue. In an effort to help us not to be deceived, God has purposely instructed us in 1 Thessalonians 5:21 NASB to "Examine everything carefully . . . and to hold fast to that which is good" By Knowing God's will and the message of the gospel of Christ in the Bible, we have the means, that is, the "knowledge" to compare and examine carefully the teachings of any church. If the church's teachings do not parallel the exact message of Christ and the Bible, then they cannot be from the same source that produced it, that is, God. Perversion can be easily detected by the one abiding in Christ *with biblical knowledge.*

However, for lack of interest, the demonic influence and the direction the world culture is headed, most people are no longer reading the Bible as God specifically instructed us. The reality of acquiring "faith and belief" today for many good and sincere individuals around the world, is to just attend a religious organization they feel "comfortable" with and let the "church" teach them! Their religious church leaders are looked upon by their followers as "professionals," as "trustworthy," as having been schooled and trained in biblical knowledge, salvation, and knowing the will of our God. They are thought of in the highest regard and trusted to have the training and expertise to accurately convey the will of God and the true way to salvation.

This is what good people naturally expect from their religious leaders. They expect to hear and receive the truth, the pure unadulterated truth as God provided to us in the Bible. But are they all receiving it? The answer is, regrettably, no. Many of the larger religions preach varied and strange teachings and the traditions of men that run absolutely contrary to God's message and the gospel of Christ in the Holy Bible. Here are just a few examples:

- Religions that preach that eternal salvation is *only* attainable through *their* religion

- Religions that preach that salvation is *earned* by doing "good works"

- Religions that do not believe that the Bible is the inerrant Word of God

- A religion that rewrites and creates its own "bible" to "fit" their own beliefs and teachings

- Religions that preach that faith in and obedience to Christ are not necessary for eternal salvation

- Religions claiming a "divine authority" and full rights to fabricate and preach false doctrines that are not scriptural, and yet still carry on "godly business" in a manner inconsistent with the teachings of the Bible

- Religions that preach eternal punishment does not really exist, and that hell's all pagan teaching

- Religions that allow the ways of the world and its culture to influence and steer the church in a direction that is diametrically opposed to God's will in Scripture

- Religions that completely deny the deity and authority of Jesus Christ!

- Religions that preach their doctrine and the *requirement of* "penance," rather than the Scriptural requirement of *repentance*, thereby shutting tight the door of salvation to all of their many followers

- Religions that approve and encourage prayers for the dead that are contrary to God's Word

- Religions that promote prayer and worship to the "Blessed Virgin Mary" or other "saints"

- The many religions, including the bigger denominations, that preach a different and varied gospel, contrary to the teachings of the gospel of Christ in the Bible

- Religions that claim their priests and leaders can forgive sins

- Religious "extremists" inflicting undue harm in the name of Allah

- The religious doctrine of purgatory. This disrespects the finished work of our Lord Jesus that He did on the cross for man. Should we sin, He is faithful to forgive us if we repent and confess them to Him. The Bible clearly states that there is no condemnation to those who are in Christ. Purgatory is a religious doctrine of man

- Religions ignoring *and* violating God's law that marriage is the uniting of one man and one woman. The only way to determine if something is truly right is to examine it in the revealing light of God's Holy Word. Only our loving Creator has the right to define the marriage relationship.

- The Roman Inquisition marked by the severity of punishment, and the fact that Rome did not readily give us the Bible, but rather did all in her power to keep it from us and retained it under the seal of a dead language.

- The belief that becoming a member of any religion in the world and observance of its traditions allows man to find the way of eternal salvation and arrive at eternal salvation

- Religions that preach they are giving every lost person who ever lived and deceased, the chance of salvation through certain religious rituals that are contrary to Scripture and the gospel of Christ (as by baptism of the dead).

- Religions that claim their leader or high priest is infallible

It is both clear and evident that many churches including Christian denominations have deviated and violated biblical Scripture in one form or another. The ministry of religion and priesthood has always posed as *the* "authorized representatives" of God in this world. However, Satan has deeply influenced many of these ministries and injected false doctrines contrary to the Biblical word, doctrines the ministers have taught the people and confused them. Christ's apostles taught the truth, but it was not long after their death until the devil found clergymen conceited, who thought they could preach more than the inspired apostles of Jesus Christ.

As a result, for some, the clergy has become instruments in the hands of the gods of this world, Satan the devil, who has used them to blind the minds of people and to prevent them from understanding God's true word and way to eternal salvation. God said, "The whole world lies *under the sway* of the wicked one" (1 John 5:19 NKJV). The tragic result, says God, is that "They die for lack of instruction, for lack of understanding, ..Lack of *true* knowledge" (Proverbs 5:23; 10:21 NASB; Job 36:12 AMPC). "My people are destroyed because they don't know Me" (Hosea 4:6 NLT).

People worldwide have been deceived about God. They have been deceived about the Bible. They have been deceived about God's Laws and instructions. They have bought into Satan's lies and deception, and as a result, they are being *eternally destroyed*. For this reason, we must come to recognize and understand that the ultimate criterion for determining the importance and validity of anything pertaining to life, God or Salvation is the Holy Bible.

The Holy Bible is God's plain spoken instruction book from God to man. It is a book to be applied. It commands *supreme attention* **above** any church or religious organization in the world. To place greater credence and trust on man and religion over Christ and the Bible is a fatal mistake of eternal consequences. It absolutely violates God's clear and direct instructions because it can ultimately lead a follower into deception, -and all without him even knowing it! **Peter and the Apostles stated**: "If we have to choose between obedience to God and obedience to any human authority, then we must obey God" (Acts 5:29 VOICE).

God's laws and loving instructions are for *our own* direct benefit! Why would you ever place both yourself and your families *ultimate eternal destiny* in the faith and hands of man and religion who cannot save you, over God's Word in the Bible that can? Especially when the Bible is the ONLY book in the world that has been proven in three area's, historically, archeologically and validated by God's seal of hundreds of fulfilled divine prophecies? Remember, God has said; My people die for lack of instruction. Would it not therefore be prudent to seek guidance and instruction *directly* from Almighty God's Holy book the Bible, the *genuine source* for attaining truth, and wisdom and salvation? We are clearly instructed and advised in His book "That your faith should NOT rest on the wisdom of men, but on the Power of God" (1 Corin. 2:5 NASB).

Recognize there are many people who claim to represent God or claim to be Christ's disciples but have little or no love for His Word or message of truth in the Bible. With thousands of *different* faiths, religions are becoming more like big business. They will do whatever it takes to market a "more appealing" and different gospel in an effort to lure people through their doors, and all without fully complying with Christ and the Bible. It is truly tragic and the influence of the devil himself that there is so much deceptive teaching and error being preached by man. This deception will cause many to lose out on eternal salvation. The Bible forewarned the world: "See to it that no one takes you captive through philosophy and empty deception, according to the traditions of men . . . rather than according to *Christ*" (Col. 2:8 NASB).

All religions that have rejected the headship and teachings of Christ, and select their own man-made doctrines and beliefs instead of submitting themselves to the will and Word of Christ are *false* religions. Scripture says, "Have no fellowship with the unfruitful works of darkness, but rather expose them" (Eph. 5:11 NKJV).

A religion that contradicts or is different from the Bible, or that leads people away from the truth of Christ as found in the gospel of Christ, is a false religion. Turn away from it!

God's warning: Perversion of the Gospel

"But there are some who trouble you and want to pervert the gospel of Christ" [through false religions and teachings] (Gal. 1:7 NKJV). "But even if we, or an angel from Heaven, should preach to you a gospel contrary to the one we preached to you, let him be accursed. As we have said before, so now I say again: If *anyone*, [regardless of reputation or credentials], is preaching to you a gospel *contrary* to the one you received [in Scripture], let him be accursed" (Gal. 1:8-9 ESV). "For such men are false apostles, deceitful workers, disguising themselves as apostles of Christ" (2 Cor. 11:13 NASB).

God has warned us in the strongest possible language of these purveyors of error and heresy who want to distort and preach another gospel contrary to Scripture. Believe it or not, many of today's religions have lost, changed, twisted, and perverted the true gospel of Christ to suit their beliefs. Why isn't the true gospel of our Lord Jesus Christ being preached by all the churches today? Do not be deceived! With so many different religions and cults in America alone, there are many false gospels being preached.

Hatred fuels Satan's actions. Satan has an intense and burning hostility against God and all that God loves. Since ancient times, Satan has attempted to neutralize God's people from ever connecting with God. He deceives leaders of religions and uses them to pull entire groups of innocent people into falsehood and away from Christ. He is immensely successful at deception, as evident by the thousands of religions that believe his lies. People who reject the gospel of Christ and biblical authority lead whole denominations with millions and millions of followers astray.

By infiltrating misguided believers into "Christian" places of higher learning, the "father of lies" has successfully reproduced thousands of pastors and priests who have lost their faith in Scripture and now take their lead from the trending patterns of Satan's own world system. Religions led by these people cannot and will not point to Christ because they do not believe in the gospel of Christ. These religions that lack the true biblical compass for direction drift further and further from biblical truth with essentially no constraint. Once a religion authorizes man to generate religious doctrines that have equal or greater authority with the Word of God, almost anything can happen. Religious cults and leaders can then lure people into their religion by making "wonderful promises" that are contrary to the gospel of Christ. This is *extremely dangerous* because they cause many people to follow them, thereby rejecting God's only way to salvation. Of such religious teachers the Bible warns, "There are many rebellious men, ..deceivers, ..teaching things they should not teach, ..those who are defiled and unbelieving. They 'profess' to know God, but by *their* deeds they deny *Him*" (Titus 1:10-11,15-16 NASB). Today, as never before in the past, the spirit of the Antichrist is invading our world and our sanctuaries and at an accelerating pace. Religion without Christ's true message is the tool of Satan to draw people into his realm.

As a result, hundreds of millions are pinning their full faith and belief (and eternal salvation) to a product of man-made doctrines and beliefs. And unfortunately, many are being deceived. These types of religions are commonplace today.

They use the "guise" of Christianity while denying the deity and blood sacrifice of Jesus, thereby denying eternal life to all their members. They claim to be based on Christian doctrine, yet differ *substantially* from established orthodox theology. Their religious leaders and preachers have their own set of books and religious literature explaining the church doctrines, traditions, and beliefs that must be preached, but only as interpreted by *their* religion.

Against all credible scholarship and against the very words of God's Scripture, Jesus is very often discredited and denied His authority by religions and "downgraded" to just a teacher or an angel. But exactly whose teaching does God say we should remember? Does He say "religious" teachings? No, not at all! He says in Colossians 3:16 TLB, "Remember what *Christ* taught, let *His* words enrich your lives and make you wise." Why? Because we are told in John 13:13 NASB that Christ is our teacher. Scripture says "Let our roots grow down in Him" (Col. 2:7). Scripture teaches "that our determined purpose is that we know Him, that we may progressively become more deeply and intimately acquainted with Him, perceiving and recognizing and understanding the wonder of His person more strongly and more clearly" (Phil. 3:10 AMPC)

Any denomination that discredits the gospel of Christ or God's Word the Bible is telling another lie of Satan, which is designed to cause many people to be *eternally lost* in hell. The Bible speaks of Satan as the devil, the one "who deceives the whole world" (Rev. 12:9 NASB). "Don't give the Devil that kind of foothold in your life" (EPH. 4:27 MSG).

Satan's primary goal is to separate man from God and what the Bible says. Jesus explains, "Those by the wayside are the ones who hear; then the devil comes and takes away the Word out of their hearts, lest they should believe and be saved" (Luke 8:12 NKJV). Satan does this by taking God's Word out of the hearts of these people in the denominational churches and replacing it with false man-made doctrines and creeds that run contrary to God's instruction and the gospel of Christ. And because of this, all the people in their denominations remain lost. Jesus warns us to "Beware of false prophets who come to you in sheep's clothing, but inwardly are ravenous wolves" (Matt. 7:15 NASB). A shallow knowledge of the Bible is one reason we are particularly vulnerable. Without a deep knowledge of God's Word the Bible, we are truly "sheep among the ravenous wolves." We can easily be deceived.

When church evangelists and pastors teach that Christ and His gospel message do not demand His followers to repent of breaking God's laws, or follow with obedience and a change of heart, but rather preach another false gospel, they are taking away from God's Word and the gospel. As Scripture says in (Jude 4 KJ21), they teach a perverted message of Christ by " . . . turning the grace of our God into licentiousness" [permission to continue to sin and break God's commandments], which teaches lies about the true gospel without shame." The apostle Paul in the Bible warned about man's "counterfeit" Christianity when he said the following:

"You seem so gullible: You believe whatever anyone tells you even if he is preaching about another Jesus than the one we preached . . . or shows you a different way to be saved. And you swallow it all" (2 Cor. 11:4 TLB). These perverted gospel messages being preached are bad news to its followers who are being deceived. It seems that nobody wants to look into their Bible and see just what it *really does say*, but rather follow man and religion and their false teachings, causing all to fall.

As Scripture states, these false prophets and preachers appear as innocent ministers of righteousness as they promote their counterfeit faiths with false teachings, but spiritually, they are very dangerous. Spiritually, they are out for the kill. God's Word says, "There will be false teachers among you, who will secretly introduce destructive heresies, even denying the Master. . . . Many will follow their shameful ways, and because of them the way of truth will be maligned" (2 Peter 2:1-2 AMP). These "destructive heresies" are all the false teachings of many religious denominations worldwide, which hundreds of millions and possibly *billions* may follow into eternal damnation.

Surely, if God permitted our Bibles to suddenly talk and speak out, the Bibles would cringe and cry and grieve in sorrow for man's disbelief and gross violations of Scripture. They would become soaked with tears of blood and water. They would certainly cry out, declaring man's transgressions and saying, "Come here and listen, O nations of the earth. Let the world and everything in it hear My Words" (Isa. 34:1 NLT). "Listen, O My people, to My instruction; Incline your ears to the words of My mouth" (Ps. 78:1 NASB). "My son, Keep My words and treasure My commandments within you" (Prov. 7:1 NASB). And if the Bible could speak, it would surely say, "Do not trust in princes, in mortal man, in whom there is no salvation" (Ps. 146:3 NASB). "Your faith should not rest on the wisdom and rhetoric of men, but on the Power of God" (1 Corin. 2:5 AMP). "We must obey God rather than men" (Acts 5:29 ESV).

May God stop the massive perversion of His gospel that we see in our midst today. You need to understand *His* message: It is absolutely necessary to believe the Gospel of Christ to be saved! God does not want anyone to lose their eternal salvation. God is calling on all people to wake up, *to gain knowledge*, to recognize that no man and no religion can provide salvation. God says, "My people are destroyed for lack of knowledge" (Hosea 4:6. NASB). He's right! Because of a lack of knowledge of biblical truth, false doctrines have sprouted up and become widespread, and have misled millions of people into a false sense of security that has caused them to close their eyes to the truth of God's Word. Do not be deceived! Listen to what God is telling us! "You can enter God's Kingdom only through the narrow gate. The highway to hell is broad, and its gate is wide for the many who choose that way. But the gateway to [everlasting] life is very narrow and the road is difficult, and only a few ever find it" (Matt. 7:13-14 NLT). Take the time, therefore, and read the Bible. Listen to Christ, abide in His Word, and gain your salvation.

Please, do your own due diligence and choose wisely. Know that God is calling on all of us and that time is quickly running out. "Only conduct yourselves in a manner worthy of the gospel of Christ" (Phil. 1:27 NASB). God endorsed only one book for the study of Scripture, and that is the Bible. It provides man a line of defense against false teachings. God said, "This book of the law shall not depart from your mouth, but you shall meditate on it day and night" (Josh. 1:8 NASB). He wants you to know it for your own benefit!

God's divine book has survived thousands of years, has been proven and validated by historians, by scholars, by cross-checking thousands of manuscripts, and sealed as the Word of God through fulfilled prophecy. Make it your life, therefore, to pray and to read God's Word, that you may grow in the grace and knowledge of our Lord Jesus Christ. Remember, however, that the Holy Spirit is *necessary to understand* spiritual truth, and that the Holy Spirit is given only to those who truly *believe* and *obey* God (see Acts 5:32 NASB).

Therefore, the greater your obedience to God, the greater your wisdom and understanding of the Bible. God said, "Getting wisdom is the wisest thing you can do!" (Prov. 4:7 NLT). And God's instructions are meant solely for your benefit. He wants you to get the pure and unadulterated word directly from *Him*. Without the biblical knowledge God wants you to get, your ability to quickly detect deception and truth is removed, along with the promised blessings that come only with trusting and abiding in God's Word the Bible. For this reason, it is of utmost importance that we *always* give greater credence and place our allegiance with God and His Word over man and religion.

All Christians need to find a church for fellowship and worship, but due diligence is absolutely required in determining if the church's beliefs are truly in line with the Bible and the gospel of Christ. Does the church encourage its followers to bring their Bibles to church? Does the church provide Bible teaching that is in sync with Scripture? It is absolutely imperative that the God of our Bible, and specifically the gospel of Christ, always remain the gold standard and reference standard for all biblical teachings and belief.

There is nothing in our lifetime that is of greater importance and urgency than making sure we are connected to the right church that is dispensing God's true and unadulterated Word. Just as we would wisely seek professional advice and counsel in other critical matters of life, it's just as important, and even more so, in making absolutely certain we seek the right church in hearing God's *true, authentic Word.* "Why," you ask? For the reason of not being deceived by man and religion and losing out on eternal salvation. Understand that Satan, in his attempt to deceive, will create religions without a redeemer, will build churches without Jesus, will promise salvation without the gospel of Christ, and will call for worship without the Word of God. Don't let yourself be deceived. Don't be misled. Don't get hurt.

Unlike other professions in America, such as engineering, real estate, electrical, plumbing, accounting, legal, medical, and so on, where there is strong adherence to the rule of law, to high ethics, accountability, and legal recourse should one be deceived and wronged, there exists no such safeguards or protection in the realm of religion and its teachings of salvation. If you and your family have been wronged and deceived, which results in your loss of eternal salvation, you are on your own! You will have no recourse on judgment day. And don't even think for a minute you can make a defense on judgement day and say to God, Please Lord, hold on, don't judge me and my family for my choice of church. With so many church's how could I possibly have know which church preaches the true gospel of Christ? And God will immediately respond by saying; I didn't say believe on the church. "<u>I said believe on the Lord Jesus Christ and you will be saved</u>" (Acts 16:31). You had the Prophetic Word made more sure, to which you would have done well to pay attention (2 Peter 1:19 NASB). You would have learned that I said; "If any man is preaching to you a gospel contrary to that which you received [in My Word], let him be accursed" (Galatians 1:9). You were to "learn from Me" (Matt. 11:29 NASB). Therefore, protect your interests, your family, and your children, and seek the Word of God that teaches the true gospel of Christ. "Seek from the book of the Lord, and read" (Isa. 34:16 NASB). "*This* book of the law [The Bible] shall not depart from your mouth, but you shall meditate on it day and night, so that you may be careful to do according to all that is written in it; for then, you will make your way prosperous, and then, you will have success" (Joshua 1:8 NASB).

No religious leader, entity or head of state can claim to have the sole rights and "infallible" teaching authority from God. Furthermore no religion on this planet is equal to or above the inerrant Word of God for teaching and instruction. The Bible clearly speaks of only one abiding, infallible guide left by God for His church. It is the written word of God declaring that "All Scripture is inspired by God and profitable for teaching, for reproof, for correction, and for training in righteousness" (2 Tim. 3:16 NASB). In the following opening address below it is clear that Paul Christ's apostle, is angry with what is going on among the churches and people with regard to those rejecting the biblical message and turning to other false preachings as is the case today!

Paul said, "I am astonished and extremely irritated that you are so quickly shifting your allegiance and deserting Him who called you by the grace of Christ, for a different even contrary gospel; which is really not another [gospel]; but there are some [people masquerading as teachers] who are disturbing and confusing you [with a misleading, counterfeit teaching], and want to distort the gospel of Christ twisting it into something which it absolutely is not]. But even if we, or an angel from Heaven, should preach to you a gospel contrary to that which we preached to you, let him be condemned to destruction! As we have said before, so I now say again, if anyone is preaching to you a gospel different from that which you have received from us, let him be condemned to destruction! (Galatians 1:6-9 AMP). People are to turn to God and the "word of His grace" for their guidance in determining the truth not by who said it, but by comparing it with the gospel already received, the gospel recorded for us in Scripture. (Galatians 1:8-9; see also Acts 17:11).

As Scripture teaches, "Keep the charge of the Lord your God, to walk in *His* ways, to keep *His* statutes, *His* commandments, *His* ordinances, *His* testimonies" (1 Kings 2:3 NASB). "Give attention to reading of Scripture . . . be absorbed in them". "Pay close attention. . . . Persevere in these things, for as you do this you will *ensure* salvation both for yourself and for those who hear you" (1 Tim. 4:13, 15-16 NASB).

What history has clearly demonstrated is that, when any source of authority is treated as being of equal weight with God's Word in the Bible, that second authority always ends up superseding the Holy Scripture and then imposing its own new found beliefs and doctrines upon their followers. Religions then in an attempt to "enforce" their beliefs will sometimes pronounce a curse (or death) upon those who reject their authority and teachings. However, the Bible in (Galatians 1:8-9) clearly reserves that curse for those who would teach a different or varied gospel contrary from what had already been given and recorded in the New Testament.

God's Word says; "If any man is preaching to you a gospel contrary to that which you received, let him be accursed"! In other words, we are not to rest solely on church sayings as being God's word and *final authority*, because the Bible teaches it is Scripture, that is to be used as a measuring stick and reference standard to determine truth from error. Only God's "inerrant word" that "endureth for ever" is final authority. Not man nor religion. Remember, God commanded us, "Seek from the book of the Lord, and read" (Isa. 34:16 NASB). "Listen, O my people, to My instruction; incline your ears to the words of My mouth" (Ps.78:1 NASB).

We give no glory to God, and show no respect for God by attending and participating in a religion that blatantly differs from His holy book the Bible, and fails to teach and abide by the true inerrant Word of God and gospel of Jesus Christ.

197

CHAPTER 38

What Are the Consequences for the Wicked and Those Who Forget God?

N ote: What you are about to read here may initially shock you. Please keep reading and understand that the purpose here is not to offend but to inform. The Scripture is clear and absolute about the magnificent promises and gift that awaits those who receive God's gracious and free offer through Jesus Christ. However, the Bible is also equally clear about the consequences of rejecting that offer. This question is about God's future judgment and a Scriptural warning of what is and what is to come.

"The Lord is known by the judgment He executes; The wicked is snared in the works of his own hands. The wicked shall be turned into hell, and all the nations that forget God" (Ps. 9:16-17 NKJV). "For a fire is kindled in mine anger, and shall burn unto the lowest hell" (Deut. 32:22 KJV). It is a "lake of fire" (Rev.20:14 NKJV). It is "the blackness of darkness for ever" (Jude 13 NKJV). "And the smoke of their torment ascends forever and ever; and they have no rest day or night" (Rev. 14:11 NKJV).

"When the Lord Jesus will be revealed from Heaven with His mighty angels in flaming fire, dealing out retribution to those who do not [seek to] know God and to those who do not obey the Gospel of our Lord Jesus [by choosing not to believe and respond to Him], these will pay the penalty of eternal destruction" (2 Thess. 1:7-9 NASB). "And whosoever was not found written in the Book of Life was cast into the lake of fire" (Rev. 20:15, KJV) "And they will be tormented day and night forever and ever" (Rev. 20:10 NASB). "In that place there will be weeping [over sorrow and pain] and grinding of teeth" (Matt. 22:13 AMP; Luke 13:28, NASB). " . . . in undergoing the punishment of eternal fire" (Jude 7 NASB). And "the cowards, those who *refuse to believe*, who do evil things, who kill, who sin sexually, who do evil magic, who worship idols, and who tell lies, -all these will have a place in the lake of burning sulfur" (Rev. 21:8 NCV).

"For God did not spare even the angels who sinned, but threw them into hell" (2 Peter 2:4 TLB). If you are an unbeliever or a scoffer at the truth of our Lord, Jesus asks, "How will you escape the sentence of hell?" (Matt. 23:33 NASB). If your soul is obsessed with the pursuit of money; if you are a person of wealth without the true riches of God; if you are a person on a voyage of life without prayer, without concern for your immortal good, your God, or your eternal destination, *please*, hear carefully what Scripture says: "Hell hath enlarged herself, and opened her mouth without measure: and their glory, and their multitude, and their pomp, and he that rejoiceth, shall descend into it" (Isa. 5:14 KJV).

The mind of the unsaved man is given some very uncomplimentary words in God's book. They are "blinded" by Satan (see 2 Cor. 4:4 KJV), "defiled" (see Titus 1:15 KJV), "devoted to worthless pursuits" (see Eph. 4:17 VOICE), "darkened" (see Eph. 4:18 NKJV), and "reprobate" (see Rom. 1:28 KJV).

If you have wanted to be a Christian, lingering many years on the edge of the kingdom, looking through the gates but never ready to enter, intending, but not performing, often wishing, but still postponing, hoping but not acting, then this Scripture is to you: "How shall we escape if we neglect so great a salvation?" (Heb. 2:3 KJ21). In all the world, Jesus possessed the most compassionate and loving heart that ever beat in man, and yet He spoke of hell, He warned of hell, and He throughly described hell. In Jesus' public ministry of approximately forty-two months, there are many recorded instances of Jesus speaking about hell. No doubt He probably warned of hell thousands of times. Jesus speaks more than anyone else about hell. He says, "The highway to hell is broad, and its gate is wide for the many who choose that way" (Matt. 7:13 NLT). In Revelation 21:8 have you noticed that even the "unbelievers" are included with all the morally perverted people on the list? You don't have to be a great sinner to get into the lake of fire, you can be merely an unbelieving sinner. Jesus has warned us over and over of the eternal consequences of sin and unbelief. The issue is so serious, the Bible refers to hell well over a hundred times!

Read what our Lord says about hell in Mark 9:43-48, Matthew 13:41-42, 13:49-50, 25:41, 46. Hell is an everlasting, *conscious* punishment and a reality of God's infinite justice upon the wicked and the souls of unbelieving persons. Oh, you who may be unsaved and believeth not. *Please,* turn about with all haste. *Time is truly of the essence.* "Seek ye Lord while He may be found, call ye upon Him while He is near: Let the wicked forsake his way, and the unrighteous man his thoughts; and let him return unto the Lord, and he will have mercy upon him; and to our God, for he will abundantly pardon" (Isa. 55:6-7 AKJV). Please read Matthew 25. How terribly tragic to go through life, expecting to be saved, only to be rejected by the just and righteous Judge in the day when mercy will be *past!*

Scripture says: "Behold, now is the favorable time; behold, now is the day of salvation" (2 Cor. 6:2 ESV). For "The Lord will by no means leave *the guilty* unpunished" (see Nah. 1:3 NASB, Rom. 1:18, Eph. 5:6, Col. 3:6, 2 Peter 2:9, Rev. 6:17, 14:10). Every true church of God and follower of Christ must see this present time as an opportunity to warn the lost about God's wrath against sin, the coming day of judgment, and the dangers of hell. Religions that make much to-do about God's love but fail to preach His role as a judge and the reality of hell will prevent people from understanding God's hatred of sin and the future punishment for wrongdoing.

Comment: Satan has both strong and obvious motives for fueling our denial of eternal punishment. He wants unbelievers to permanently reject God without fear. He wants Christians to be unmotivated in reading the Bible and learning the truth, and he wants God to receive no glory for Christ's life-saving and redemptive work. Today there are books and religions that deny hell. There are also countless groups, religious and secular, that will assure you heaven is your destination or that it can be attained by your good works and abstention from certain sins.

They can be persuasive, often quoting the Bible out of context. They argue that Christians should take the higher road of Christ's love. But this perspective *overlooks* a very conspicuous reality: That Jesus Himself explains and warns more than anyone else about hell in the Bible. Truly, we need to appreciate our Lord's loving message to us. And like Christ, the most loving thing we can do for our family and friends is to share with them about the road that leads to destruction and tell them about the road that leads to life.

Question: While it may be upsetting, would we think it "unloving" if a doctor told us we had a potentially fatal disease or cancer? And would the doctor not tell us if it could be cured? Why then, do we not tell unsaved people about the disease of sin and evil and how the inevitable penalty of eternal destruction can be *avoided* by the atoning sacrifice of our Lord? God loves us enough to tell us the truth, that there are only two eternal destinations after death, heaven or hell, and each is just as real and just as eternal as the other, and that we must choose the right way if we are to go to heaven.

God declares to all nations and all the people of the earth that *now* is the favorable time and *now* should be the day of salvation because no one knows what tomorrow brings. Today, God is granting still *more time* as He wishes that none should perish. But time is truly running out! For those who reject our Lord Jesus Christ there is no forgiveness anywhere else, anytime, either in this world or the next. It is only "In Him we have redemption through His blood, the forgiveness of our trespasses, according to the riches of His Grace" (Eph. 1:7 NASB). He suffered and died for you and if you reject that THEN THERE IS NO OTHER SACRIFICE FOR SIN.

If you reject Christ and refused Him as your Lord and Savior, and you put down this book and walk out across the street and get hit by a vehicle or have a heart attack and die, you will have committed the unpardonable sin permanently effecting your eternal destination, and there is *no recourse* for you. Don't make that mistake. Don't gamble that you'll have time to respond later on. God commands us, "Seek the Lord while He may be found, call upon Him while He is near" (Isaiah 55:6 NASB). Remember, He is the way, the truth and the life. He is your friend, your mediator, your redeemer and if you so chose, He can be your Savior too.

God has purposely emphasized in the very strongest possible language that they who are not saved have an urgent need of salvation and need to do it now, do it today, while it is still possible.

There is no second chance for those who passed away and rejected the free gift of salvation that Jesus offers everyone. It is then too late to reverse one's trajectory once a person dies. The unbelievers and the wicked are not given another chance. Furthermore, death in the biblical sense never means "extinction or annihilation," and not one word in Greek or Hebrew or in either Testament will be found to say it does. To preach such is a violation of Scripture. Its use is *grossly misleading* and not supported by the gospel of Christ. Death is not extinction or annihilation, and hell is not an illusion as some religions preach. If God had plans to annihilate sinful mankind, then why did Jesus come down and die for us? What did He save us from?

The Word of God clearly teaches that the suffering of the lost in hell is eternal, and that it will be a place of utter misery where the fire is not quenched. (Read Matt. 25:41, 46 KJV, Mark 9:43-46, 48 KJV, Matt. 13:41-43 NASB, Rev. 14:11 KJV, 2 Thess. 1:9 KJV, Isa. 66:24KJV, Rev. 20:10 KJV, Rev. 21:8 KJV, Matt. 18:8 KJV, Matt. 25:41 KJV, Matt. 22:13 KJV, Rev. 19:20, Jude 6-7 NKJV, and others.) These verses and so many others throughout Scripture are conclusive proof that everlasting conscious separation from God and real torment exist, and that no possible confusion of terminology can change their meaning in context.

God has made it too clear, explained it too well, and described it all too frequently for anyone to ignore. There are well over 100 warnings about judgment and eternal punishment in the Bible.

Read carefully how Jesus described the fate of the unrighteous: "But for the cowardly and unbelieving and murders and immoral persons and sorcerers and idolaters and all liars, their part will be in the lake that burns with fire and brimstone" (Rev. 21:8 NASB). "These will go away into eternal punishment, but the righteous into eternal life" (Matt. 25:46 NASB).

If you are a follower of a religion that does not teach the *unadulterated* Gospel of our Lord and Savior Jesus Christ, know that God is calling on *you*, reaching out to *you*, pleading with *you*, that you return to Him, that you listen to Him, and that you trust in Him. God is truly distressed at the number of lost and deceived, and is pleading with all people of the world, while there is still "grace and mercy and time," that we come to recognize and trust *His* Word, and that there is no salvation in man and his religion, but only through Christ Jesus.

Jesus Himself was so compelled to speak on hell and eternal punishment that He mentioned it on forty-six separate occasions in order to emphasize and forewarn of the seriousness of sin and the reality of a place of conscious punishment. In the story of the rich man and Lazarus in Luke 16:19-31, Jesus could have easily portrayed the rich man and Lazarus in another way. He could have said, for example, that when they died, their spirit left them without a body and went into a realm without sin, without pain, and without consciousness. But no, Jesus did not say that. He tells us of a different story as evidence to be *believed and trusted.* Remember, the Bible is God's book that reveals the truth of God.

Remember also that Jesus came into this world to bear witness and testify to the truth. Not to mislead and misrepresent. He would not have conveyed that message if it was not true. His words about the outcome and afterlife of the rich man and Lazarus are very clear and are meant to teach us the reality and truth of both heaven and hell.

So the decision you make about Christ in this lifetime is what determines your eternal destiny. When a person passes away, their eternal destiny is permanently set and cannot be changed. The wrongful assertion by man and religion that God is unfair to punish eternally a temporary sin, underestimates the seriousness of sin, the spiritual nature of sin, and the supreme holiness of God. They make much ado that God is all love but forget that because He is love, He is also a *just* God and requires infinite retribution upon anyone who treads on the precious blood of Christ, who is the slain lamb for lost sinners from the foundation of the world. Listen to what God has to say . . .

"Say to them, 'As I live!' declares the Lord GOD, 'I take no pleasure in the death of the wicked, but rather that the wicked turn from his way and live.'" (Ezek. 33:11 NASB). "Therefore say to them, 'Thus says the Lord of hosts, "Return to Me," declares the Lord of hosts, "that I may return to you" (Zech. 1:3 NASB).

He tells us that if we sincerely repent of our sins and ask forgiveness, and "if we confess with our mouth Jesus as Lord, and believe in our heart that God raised Him from the dead, we will be saved; For with the heart a person believes, resulting in righteousness, and with the mouth he confesses, resulting in salvation" (Rom. 10:9-10 NASB).

If you have been putting off your response, your RSVP, or if you think you can enter heaven without responding to our Lord's invitation, one day you will *surely* and *deeply* regret it. If you are an unbeliever and haven't accepted Christ as your Lord and Savior, please, *now is the time!* Scripture says, "Today I have given you the choice between life and death, between blessings and curses. Now I call on heaven and earth to witness the choice you make. Oh, that you would choose life, so that you and your descendants might live!" (Deut. 30:19 NLT). God has a permissive will and grants man a "free will," so man can decide as he pleases, and may use his choice to disobey and deny God. God is bound to always honor and respect our freedom of choice as He has done even with His angels. He will not intervene and save anyone against their will. But understand this: "God has not destined us for wrath, but for obtaining salvation through our Lord Jesus Christ, who died for us, so that whether we are awake or asleep, we will live together with Him" (1 Thess. 5:9-10 NASB).

Consider this: Our Lord so much wants us *not* to go to hell that He paid a horrific price on the cross so that we would not have to. The price has been paid! But still, we must choose. Like any gift, forgiveness can be given, but it is not ours until we choose to receive it. Just like a convicted person can be offered a pardon by the president or governor, but if he or she rejects the pardon, it is not valid. A pardon must be accepted. Likewise, Christ offers each of us the gift of forgiveness and eternal life with Him, but just because the offer is made does not automatically make it ours. To obtain it, we must choose to accept it. We are made right in God's sight only when we choose to accept it and place our faith and trust in Jesus to take away our sins.

Receiving and accepting this free gift of salvation is as simple as saying, Jesus, I acknowledge my sins and your payment for it on the cross. I turn away from my sins and repent and ask you to forgive me. I open the door to my heart and invite you to come into my life, and I place my complete trust in You alone and thank you for this free gift of eternal salvation. From that moment on, if said sincerely, He will come into your innermost being and start you on a wonderful journey toward intimacy with Christ.

It is your choice! Are you willing to follow Christ's way or your own way? Are you willing to gamble your most valuable asset, your soul, on simply your feelings or what "religion" dictates as "truth"? Would it not be far more prudent to base your beliefs on an established book divinely inspired by our Creator that has been scrutinized by thousands of scholars, historians, and the like, and yet found to be true? The decision here is yours.

However, if you make the decision to decline Christ's offer of eternal salvation and reject Him, God will let you have your way. You are free to choose, but you are *not* free to choose the eternal consequence of your choice. God has clearly forewarned us of the great danger that lies ahead if we so choose to go our own way and not live together with Him, so we are without excuse!   Please, choose wisely!

Listen carefully to Scripture's warning against neglecting salvation: "For this reason we must pay much closer attention to what we have heard, so that we do not drift away from it" (Heb. 2:1 NASB). "For if we go on sinning deliberately after receiving the knowledge of truth, there no longer remains a sacrifice for our sins, but a fearful expectation of judgement, and a fury of fire that will consume the adversaries" (Heb. 10:26-27 ESV). "Just think how much more severe the punishment will be for those who turned their backs on the Son of God, and trampled on the blood of the covenant by which He made holy, and outraged the Spirit of grace *with their contempt*" (Heb. 10:29 VOICE).

Part 7

Scriptural Summary Points to Remember

- For many will come in My name to mislead many and distort the gospel of Christ. Avoid such people as these, and turn away from them.

- In whose case the god of this world has blinded the minds of the unbelievers, that they might not see the light of the gospel of the glory of Christ

- See to it that no one takes you captive through philosophy and empty deception, according to the traditions of men, rather than according to Christ.

- Do not be carried away by varied and strange teachings or you forfeit union with God! We have something *more sure*, the *Prophetic Word*, to which you do well to pay attention.

- Whosoever transgresseth, and abideth not in the doctrine of Christ, he hath *not* God.

- Remember what Christ taught, and let *His* words enrich you.

- God's instructions for salvation are very simple and very clear; they are all straightforward to him that understands.

- For My people are destroyed for lack of knowledge.

- "Everyone who doesn't continue to teach what Christ taught doesn't have God" "Anyone who does not stay with the teachings of Christ, but goes beyond it, does not have God" (2 John 9 GW, GNT).

- So know Scripture *well enough* to identify what is true and authentic and what is perverse and contrary to Christ's teachings. Do not allow yourself to be deceived and lose out on eternal salvation.

- Behold, now is the favorable time; behold, *now* is the day of salvation while there is still grace and time and mercy.

- The Lord will by no means leave the guilty unpunished.

- The eternal consequence and warnings of unrepentant sin and unbelief are so serious that the Bible refers to hell well over 100 times.

- "And these go away into eternal punishment," Jesus said of the unrighteous, "but the righteous into eternal life."

- Remember, "Jesus is the only One who can save people. No one else in the world is able to save us" (Acts 4:12 NCV). Scripture asks: "How shall we escape if we neglect so great a salvation?"

PART 8

Christ's Return and His Divine Message to Mankind

CHAPTER 39

Is He Coming Back, What Are We To Do? What Is The Rapture & The Tribulation?

"Behold, I am coming quickly" (Rev. 3:11 NKJV). ". . . that hour which is about to come upon the whole world, to test those who dwell on the earth" (Rev. 3:10 NASB). "For the day of the Lord is coming; Surely it is near" (Joel 2:1 NASB). "Yet even now," declares the Lord, "Return to Me with all your heart, and with fasting, weeping and mourning" (Joel 2:12 NASB). "Turn to Me and be saved, all the ends of the earth; For I am God, and there is no other" (Isa. 45:22 NASB). "The Lord is not slow about His promise, as some count slowness, but is patient toward you, not wishing for any to perish but for all to come to repentance" (2 Peter 3:9 NASB).

Comment: The message of the second coming of Jesus is so critical, so important, that it is mentioned over 300 times in the New Testament. However, Jesus said, "But about that day or hour [of His return] no one knows . . . , but only the Father" (Matt. 24:36 NIV). The Bible makes it clear that only those who have the Holy Spirit living in them, that is, those who truly believe in Jesus as Savior, can understand the "nature of the times" that mark His return (see 1 Thess. 5:2-6).

God deals with sin and unbelief in one of two ways, either in grace or in wrath. A person is under either the grace of God or the wrath of God. There is no other option available. To be under the grace of God is truly a glorious thing and means you have the promise that one day soon Jesus will appear and take you out of this world in an event called the Rapture, before He deals wrathfully with rebellion on earth (see 1 Thess. 4:17).

What is the Rapture? The rapture of the church is the mechanism, the miraculous event in which God "snatches up" the church *[all believers in Christ]* from the earth in order to make way for His righteous judgement to be poured out on the earth during the Tribulation period. The rapture will involve an instantaneous transformation of our bodies to fit us for eternity. "We know that, when He [Christ] appears, we shall be like Him, because we shall see Him just as He is" (1 John 3:2 NASB). Believers who have died will have their bodies resurrected and, along with believers who are still living, will meet the Lord in the air. This will occur in a moment, in the twinkling of an eye.

Paul an apostle of Christ explained: "For we say this to you by the Lord's own word, that we who are still alive and remain until the coming of the Lord, will in no way precede those [believers] who have fallen asleep [in death]. For the Lord Himself will come down from heaven with a shout of command, with the voice of the archangel and with the [blast of the] trumpet of God, and the dead in Christ will rise first. Then we who are alive and remain [on earth] will *simultaneously* be caught up (snatched away or raptured) together with them [the resurrected ones] in the clouds to meet the Lord in the air, and so we will *always* be with the Lord! Therefore comfort and encourage one another with these words" (1 Thess. 4:15-18 AMP).

The rapture will constitute the fulfillment of prophecy and the end of the church age on earth, wherein all believers will be taken up to meet the Lord. Those that remain on earth, all the unbelievers, will enter the period of God's wrath called the great Tribulation. The Tribulation is a seven year period of worsening conditions, the wrath of God against the wicked. During the Tribulation the Antichrist will come to rule and be at the center of the Tribulations evil. Because God's return is imminent we are all on a collision course with destiny and we cannot afford to be ignorant.

Christ's coming is fast approaching!! All the Biblical prophecies which must be completed before His return for the church have been fulfilled. Our Lord will descend with a shout and the trumpet of God. And the church of all true believers in Christ, living and dead, will suddenly meet the Lord in the air and all in a blink of an eye. Like an eager bride, the church awaits for the climatic unification with her Groom. The only way we can know about the mystery of the rapture is by studying what the New Testament prophets had to say. This was revealed to the apostle Paul who said; "Listen very carefully, I tell you a mystery [a secret truth decreed by God and previously hidden, but now revealed]; we will not all sleep [in death], but we will all be changed [wondrously transformed], in a moment, in the twinkling of an eye, at [the sound of] the last trumpet call. For a trumpet will sound, and the dead [who believed in Christ] will be raised imperishable, and we will be [completely] changed [wondrously transformed]. For this perishable [part of us] must put on the imperishable [nature], and this mortal [part of us that is capable of dying] must put on immortality [which is freedom from death]" (1 Corin. 15:51-53 AMP).

There are two reasons for the rapture. First, it is because Jesus brings us home. It is the *fulfillment of His promise to all believers* that we are "to obtain an inheritance which is imperishable and undefiled, and will not fade away, reserved in Heaven for you, who are protected by the power of God through faith, for a salvation ready to be revealed in the last time" (1 Peter 1:3-5 NASB). Jesus said; "In My Father's house are many mansions; if it were not so, I would have told you. I go to prepare a place for you. And if I go and prepare a place for you, I will come again and receive you to Myself; that were I am, *there* you may be also" (John 14:2-3 NKJV).

The rapture is a glorious event we should all be longing for. And thereafter we will be in God's presence forever. The second reason for the rapture is the *rescue of God's people from the wrath to come in* the great Tribulation. God has not appointed His wrath to be poured out upon the church of true believers because His wrath has *already* been satisfied, for they have placed their faith and trust in Christ and Jesus took the wrath of God for them on the cross. As a result, the wrath of God that is to be poured out is on the *unrepentant and unregenerate* world, and will be unlike anything that the world has ever seen (see Matthew 24:21).

Oh God will chastise His people, His church of true believers, but He will never pour His wrath upon them. God said; "Because you have patiently obeyed Me despite the persecution, therefore I will protect you from the time of Great Tribulation, which will come upon the world to test everyone alive" (Rev. 3:10 TLB). The church is the bride of Christ and the dearest object in the entire universe to our Lord and Savior. He will not beat up His bride in wrath. Rather He loves us! He says, "Look, I am coming soon! Hold tightly to the little strength you have - so that no one will take away your crown" (Rev. 3:11 TLB). He wants what's best for us. What sane and loving husband would ever pour out his wrath upon his bride just before the marriage supper?

The Bible *promises* over and over that those who have already accepted Jesus Christ as Lord and Savior will be delivered from God's wrath. God tells us "We shall be saved from the wrath of God through Him" (Rom. 5:9 NASB). For the Bible states we are "To wait for His Son from heaven . . . that is Jesus, who rescues us from the wrath to come" (1 Thess. 1:10 NASB). That promise (to His chosen) is repeated again: "For God has not destined us for wrath, but to obtaining salvation through our Lord Jesus Christ" (1 Thess. 5:9 ESV).

However, those under God's wrath because they have not asked for forgiveness of sins and believed in our Lord and Savior and the gospel of Christ, will stay behind and experience a wrath unlike anything the world has ever seen. This shall happen during a period the Bible calls the Tribulation.

What is the Tribulation? The Tribulation period described in the Bible is a time of divine indignation against the nations and people that have rejected our Lord. The horrors of the great Tribulation will intensify for all those who have rejected Jesus Christ, and yet He suffered so greatly and died for their sins! It will last seven terrifying years when the wrath of man, the wrath of Satan, and the wrath of almighty God will be let loose upon this earth. "For then there will be great tribulation, such as has not occurred since the beginning of the world until now, nor ever will" (Matt. 24:21 NASB).

But "He who believes in the Son has eternal life; but he who does not obey the Son will not see life, but the wrath of God abides on him" (John 3:36 NASB). It is God's very nature to love, but His love demands that evil be dealt with in justice.

The Bible teaches that God never pours out His wrath without warning. For "The Lord is not slow about His promise, as some count slowness, but is patient toward you, not wishing for any to perish but for all to come to repentance" (2 Peter 3:9 NASB). For this reason He has provided many signs to alert us of the fact that we are truly at the threshold of the Tribulation period.

All throughout recorded Biblical history God has been expressing His loving kindness and extending His mercy, grace and time to mankind. Even *during* the great 7 year Tribulation God demonstrates over and over by evidence of numerous Scriptural prophecies that His heart is to be reconciled with all He has created. In short summary, God will make every attempt to reach the lost through extreme measures by showing great wonders in the heavens and in the earth, by using two powerful witnesses (Rev. 11:3), by using 144,000 sealed bond-servants of God as witnesses that will be physically protected from all the judgements that will be hitting earth during this period (Rev. 7:3-4, 14:1), and a special angel having the everlasting gospel to preach to those who still dwell on the earth, to every nation, tribe, tongue, and people (Rev. 14:6-7). God will also have a second angel saying fallen fallen is Babylon the great, who has made all the nations drink of the wine of her immorality (Rev. 14:8), and another angel, a third one following and warning all the inhabitants in a loud voice NOT to worship the antichrist, his image or take his mark (Rev. 14:9-11).

The Bible also says that in the later days God will be pouring out His Spirit upon all flesh in an effort to get as many people saved as He possibly can (Acts 2:17-21). Most of these people who get saved during the 7 year Tribulation will have to pay the price of their life being martyred for their faith (Rev. 20:4) and for refusal to take the mark of the beast (Rev. 13:16-18; 14:9-11). Because of our Lords efforts, the Bible states that a "great multitude which no man could number" from every nation, people, race, and language will be saved and stand before the throne of God clothed in white robes (Rev. 7:9). "These are the ones who come out of the great tribulation" (Rev. 7:14)

Those who are left in this world after this 7 year Tribulation period are those who have spurned the blood of Christ. They have spurned the witness of all the prophets who came before Jesus and the apostles who came after Him. They have rejected the Bible. They have rejected the Gospel message that has been proclaimed throughout the world. In the end, those who are judged are the people who have stubbornly and utterly rejected Him. They have made it clear that they *do not want His forgiveness.* They do not want mercy or grace even when it is offered to them, and so God will take them at their word. God will not force His will on them. God does not force Himself upon anyone.

No one is saved against his will. No one is compelled to obedience who wants to be rebellious. However, the hard truth is this, all those who refuse to drink the cup of God's great salvation must drink from the bowls of His wrath (Psalm 75:8). The judgement of God is coming, and because they were given so much light but chose to stay in their darkness, their choice will be eternal. Scripture says that those who do not receive God's free gift of salvation are blotted out. "Let them be blotted out of the book of the living, and not written with the righteousness" (Psalms 69:28 KJV). "And anyone not found written in the Book of Life was cast into the lake of fire" (Rev. 20:15 NKJV) where the souls of the damned will languish for all eternity. There, separated from God's great glory, they shall remain in a permanent hopeless state of conscious agony.

So what are we to do? Where do *you* stand right now? Are you under God's wrath because you have not accepted His free gift of salvation, or are you under God's umbrella of grace because you have? Will you be amongst those who will be raptured up before God's wrath, or will you suffer it? Can you honestly say you are ready for Jesus' return?

You have a choice, a decision to make. If you have not accepted Jesus as your Lord and Savior, please, listen carefully to what He is telling us: "The time is fulfilled, and the Kingdom of God is at hand: Repent ye, and believe in the Gospel" (Mark 1:15 KJV). With all the biblical prophecies that have thus far been fulfilled with 100% accuracy, the Scriptures with stunning precision, foretells the Kingdom of God is at hand and the signs to come on the world scene about the Antichrist. The Antichrist is a person who is against Christ. He has various aliases. He is called "the lawless one" (2 Thess. 2:8 NKJV), "the evil man" (2 Thess. 2:9 NLT), "the one who brings destruction" (2 Thess. 2:3 NLT), "a master of intrigue" (Daniel 8:23 NASB) etc.

He will become the most powerful dictator the world has ever seen who persecutes, tortures and kills the people of God and will eventually lead the armies of the world into the climatic Battle of Armageddon. This "man of lawlessness" will oppose in every way Jesus Christ and at the same time displaying himself *as* being God! A quick observation of the world today reveals that lawlessness is on the rise, and will continue and increase (see 2 Tim. 3:13), and when the man of lawlessness appears on earth, he will be welcomed with open arms. Those who have rejected the true Prince of Peace, Jesus Christ, will fall for the Antichrist's empty promises of peace.

Scripture warns, "Don't be fooled by what they say. For that day will not come until there is a great rebellion against God and the man of lawlessness is revealed - the one who brings destruction" (2 Thess. 2:3 NLT). "And then the lawless one will be revealed... *that is*, the one whose coming is in accord with the activity of Satan, with all the power and signs and false wonders" (2 Thess. 2:8-9 NASB). Satan will one day soon, impersonate Christ by appearing upon the earth as a glorious being. He will deceive billions and receive the worship of the lost world. As civilization speeds closer towards its final destiny, the appearance of this powerful and destructive world dictator is clearly prophesied in scripture, and yet unrecognized and inescapable.

Remember Jesus warned us in (Matthew 24:24), that the final deception will be so persuasive, so miraculous, "that if it were possible, to even trick and mislead the saved." "He will completely fool those who are on their way to hell because they have said no to the Truth; they have refused to believe it, and love it and let it save them" (2 Thess. 2:10 TLB), "And for this cause God shall send them strong delusion, that they should believe a lie: That they all might be damned who believed not the truth" (2 Thess. 2:11-12 KJV).

Those who reject Jesus Christ and fail to repent will not do well during tribulation as God will fill their minds with delusion! Why? Because Scripture says "those are destined for eternal death because they rejected the love of truth that leads to Salvation" (2 Thess. 2:10 VOICE). "For this reason we must pay closer attention to what we have heard, so that we do not drift away from it" (Heb. 2:1 NASB). "For if we go on sinning deliberately after receiving the knowledge of truth, there no longer remains a sacrifice for sins, but a fearful expectation of judgement, and a fury of fire that will consume the adversaries" (Heb. 10:26-27 ESV).

"If we give up and turn our backs on all we've learned, all we've been given, all the truth we *now know*, we repudiate Christ's sacrifice and are left on our own to face the Judgement - and a mighty fierce judgement it will be! If the penalty for breaking the law is physical death, what do you think will happen if you turn on God's Son, spit on the sacrifice that made you whole, and insult the most gracious Spirit?" (Heb. 10:29-30 Msg). "For it had been better for them not to have known the way of righteousness, than, after they have *known it*, to turn from the holy commandment delivered to them" (2 Peter 2:21 kjv).

These individuals are those who thought they were believers, but whose profession was proven to be false. In John 15, Jesus refers to them as branches that did not remain in Him, the true Vine, and therefore did not produce any fruit. We know they are false because "by their fruits you shall know them" (Matthew 7:16, 20). True believers in Christ will exhibit the fruit of the Holy Spirit who resides within them (Galatians 5:22-23). True believers according to the Bible are overcomers, for "Everyone who is born of God overcomes the world" (1 John 5:4-5), in that they have been granted victory over the sin and unbelief of the world, and this victory is our faith. And Jesus promised us this, "He that overcometh, I will **not** blot His name out of the Book of Life" (Rev. 3:5 kjv).

God truly loves you, He created you and knows what's best for you, and has a magnificent, heavenly and eternal plan for you. Don't waste it! Don't lose it! He won't push it on you. You have a choice. Please, chose wisely. Be an overcomer. Love the truth, side with the truth, hunger for the truth, and abide in our Lord and Savior Jesus Christ. Being rooted daily in the Word of God is the *best defense* in helping you avoid being deceived, and to live a life that honors our God in the last days. In (Matthew 7:24-27), Jesus also explains that both the wise and the foolish will be experiencing tremendous storms in the last days, but that only "those who hear *and* acts upon these words of Mine" are protected and saved.

Followers of Christ who are raptured will be spared the trauma of death and all the coming disasters that will occur when the Tribulation breaks out in the world. That is indeed the reason for the rapture, its for those who love the Lord, trust the Lord and desire to be with Him. This rapture/evacuation *removes* God's chosen people to *avoid* the horrific devastation described in Scripture. "Having been justified by His blood, we shall be *saved* from the wrath of God through Him" (Rom. 5:9 NASB).

Scripture is clear that a *true* believer is kept very secure by the power of God, *sealed* for the day of redemption (Eph. 4:30). The Lord Jesus Christ proclaimed, "And I give eternal life to *them*, and they shall *never* perish; and no one shall snatch them out of My hand. My Father, who has given *them* to Me, is greater than all; and no one is able to snatch *them* out of the Father's hand. I and the Father are one" (John 10:28-30 NASB). In view of the significance of this statement, do take a moment to stop and consider this wonderful promise our loving creator has given us! Truly, we owe Him a debt of gratitude for all the loving guidance and instruction God has given us, and the promise of eternal Life with Him.

If you *sincerely* believe in all of the gospel of Christ and have accepted Jesus as your Lord and Savior, your sins have been both forgiven and forgotten. You can look forward to the glorious day when Jesus returns. Do make sure in these last days that Jesus is also Lord of *every area* of your life, so that when He returns He will find you ready. "The attitude you should have is the one that Christ Jesus had" (Philip. 2:5 GNT). "and think the same way that Jesus thought" (Philip. 2:5 CEV). "Fix your thoughts on Jesus" (Hebrews 3:1NIV). "Remember what Christ taught, and let *His* words enrich your lives and make you wise" (Colossians 3:16 TLB).

"Now learn the parable from the fig tree: when its branch has already become tender and puts forth its leaves, you know that summer is near; so, you too, when you see all these things, [see Matthew chapter

24] recognize that He is near, right at the door. Truly I say to you, this generation will not pass away until all these things take place. Heaven and earth will pass away, but My words will not pass away. But of that day and hour no one knows, not even the angels of heaven, nor the Son, but the Father alone. For the coming of the Son of Man will be just like the days of Noah. For as in those days before the flood they were eating and drinking, marrying and giving in marriage, until the day that Noah entered the ark, and they did not understand until the flood came and took them all away; so will the coming of the Son of Man be" (Matt. 24:32-39 NASB).

"Therefore you also be ready, for the Son of Man is coming at an hour you do not expect" (Luke 12:40 NKJV). "Look, I will come as unexpectedly as a thief! Blessed are all who are watching for me" (Rev. 16:15 NLT). "*Watch for My return!* This is My message to you and to everyone else" (Mark 13:37 TLB).

Take Note: Israel became a nation on May 14th, 1948. After 18 hundred centuries Israel has finally returned to her homeland as Bible prophecy had indicated. Today we are now seeing the growing hostilities of many nations being turned against her. This to, is another fulfillment of the end time prophecies. There now remains I believe no further unfulfilled prophecy that must take place before the Rapture of the church. Therefore, no Christian can afford to be ignorant of prophecy in the days we live in because the things that are prophesied here about Christ's return for His church and the Rapture are imminent.

The purpose of the Rapture is to remove the Church from the world before the wrath of God is unleashed, -the great Tribulation period! The Rapture of the Church will be a most glorious event unlike anything in the history of the world. So what are we to? May our Lord and Savior find us in His grace, in His book, turning to Him with all our heart, prepared, repentant, ready, thankful, praying and watching for His imminent coming.

CHAPTER 40

How Will It Be in the Last Days? Do You Recognize the Current Times?

"But realize this, that in the last days difficult times will come. For men will be lovers of self, lovers of money, boastful, arrogant, revilers, disobedient to parents, ungrateful, unholy, unloving, irreconcilable, malicious gossipers, without self-control, brutal, haters of good, treacherous, reckless, conceited, lovers of pleasure rather than lovers of God, holding to a form of godliness, although they have denied its power; Avoid such men as these" (2 Tim. 3:1-5 NASB). "Always learning and never able to come to the knowledge of the truth. And just as those who opposed Moses, so these men also oppose the truth, men of depraved mind, rejected in regard to the faith" (2 Tim. 3:7-8 NASB).

"You, however, continue in the things you have learned and become convinced of, knowing from whom you have learned them" (2 Tim. 3:14 NASB). And He said, "You shall love the Lord your God with all your heart, and with all your soul, and with all your mind. This is the great and foremost commandment. The second is like it, You shall love your neighbor as yourself" (Matt. 22:37-39 NASB). "And be kind to one another, tenderhearted, forgiving each other, just as God in Christ also has forgiven you" (Eph. 4:32 NASB). "Summing up: Be agreeable, be sympathetic, be loving, be compassionate, be humble. That goes for all of you, no exceptions. No retaliation. No sharp-tongued sarcasm. Instead, bless, that's your job, to bless. Here's what to do: Say nothing evil or hurtful; Snub evil and cultivate good; run after peace for all you're worth" (1 Peter 3:8 MSG).

Comment: All too often, we under estimate or fail to realize the power of a touch, a telephone call, a warm smile, a kind word, a listening ear, an honest compliment, or even the smallest act of caring and compassion for one another, all of which have the potential of turning a life around. As Scripture says, we err not knowing God's Word. The reason why more people are not saved today is because of deception and our falling away from God and His words of instruction. Satan disguises himself as an angel of light and is a master counterfeiter doing *everything* he can to blind people's eyes and close their ears to the Word of God, leading them to believe lies rather than the truth.

The Bible warns us that in the end times, people will flock to a counterfeit version of Christianity, cults that twists and perverts the true faith and Word of God. Adherents of the devil's counterfeit and spiritually adulterous faith only *appear* to worship the one true God. In reality, their hearts are far from Him. Don't be surprised if one day soon the world calls you an evil person for being a follower of Jesus Christ. Our culture today doesn't appreciate our biblical values, so some will accuse us of being bigoted or hateful or evil and intolerant. We must therefore be vigilant to maintain a pure, unadulterated gospel of Christ, free of distortion, corruption and deception. And we must make certain we remain holy, sent apart for God, and separate from the world. To give up a relationship with Christ for anyone else is a serious mistake that will be regretted for eternity.

The deceptions that Satan is already bringing to the world are only going to get *stronger*, and if you don't have a true love for the truth and are not grounded in the truth of God's Word and the gospel of Christ, then you leave yourself wide open to be deceived as so many are today. And contrary to popular thought, believing in your own chosen "truth" does not make it true for you. There is only *one* Truth, and that is our Lord Jesus Christ. Believe in Him or perish. Those who reject the truth now will be deceived and will never believe the Gospel when they hear it preached. The Bible is telling us "Behold, *now* is THE ACCEPTABLE TIME, behold, *now* is THE DAY OF SALVATION" (2 Corin. 6:2 NASB). Don't put this off! Don't wait! One day soon the Lord is coming back and if you have already rejected Him the day of opportunity will be gone. But don't think for a moment that your mere "belief" in Jesus will save you. If you have no works and no fruit in your life, then your profession of faith is dead and useless. Not one person can be "in" Jesus and not be changed by Him. Not one! If you truly believe, you will hunger for the Word and be living every day for Him and searching the Scriptures to find truth and wisdom.

Jesus is going to come for His chosen ones. Are you one of them? Do you *sincerely* believe in Him? Do you search and study the Scriptures each day? Are you obeying the gospel of Christ? Do you have a *love* for truth? Please, heed God's Scriptural warning: "He will completely fool those who are on their way to hell because they have said *no* to the Truth; they have refused to believe it and love it, and let it save them, so God will allow them to believe lies with all their hearts" (see 2 Thess. 2:10-11 TLB, NIV). They perish because they refused to love the truth and so to be saved. *Believe* therefore in Jesus! Welcome His Word. Choose Truth, love Truth, and thank God for choosing you.

CHAPTER 41

What Time Period Is God Telling Us We Are In?

"Children, this is the last hour. You heard that the enemy of Christ would appear at this time, and many of Christ's enemies have already appeared. So we know that the last hour is here" (1 John 2:18 CEV). "The end of all things is near; therefore, be of sound judgement and sober *spirit* for the purpose of prayer" (1 Peter 4:7 NASB). "Blow a trumpet in Zion and sound an alarm on My holy mountain. Let all the inhabitants of the land tremble, For the day of the Lord is coming; Surely it is near" (Joel 2:1 NASB). Jesus said, "My light will shine for you just a little longer. Walk in the light while you can, so the darkness will not overtake you" (John 12:35 NLT).

"'Yet even now,' declares the Lord. 'Return to Me with all your heart, and with fasting, weeping, and mourning'" (Joel 2:12 NASB). "Rend your hearts and not your garments and return to the Lord your God, for He is gracious and merciful, slow to anger, and abounding in loving-kindness; and He revokes His sentence of evil [when His conditions are met] (Joel 2:13 AMPC). "Believe in the Lord Jesus, and you will be saved, you and your household" (Acts 16:31 NASB). "For the day of the Lord draws near on all nations. As you have done, it will be done to you. Your dealings will return on your head" (Obad. 1:15 NASB). "Look for that blessed hope, and the glorious appearing of the great God and Savior Jesus Christ" (Titus 2:13 KJV).

"Therefore keep watch, because you do not know on what day your lord will come," (Matt. 24:42 NIV). "For this reason you also must be ready too; for the Son of Man is coming at an hour when you do not think He will" (Matt. 24:44 NASB).

Comment: God has made it abundantly clear for all of us. He has granted us time and mercy and grace to respond to Him, but time is running out. There is an urgency in His message because He is coming at an hour you don't expect! Do you understand His message? Are you ready? God loves us all and wants us to accept His precious gift, the gift of His Son Jesus Christ. The one who died on the cross that we may be saved. You see, He not only wants us to have eternal life in a glorious heaven and new earth, but have it all with *Him*, -the creator and sustainer of all things.

Oh how great is our Lord and how great is His gospel. So simple, pure and uncomplicated. And you don't have to struggle and earn your salvation. You just have to take the free gift. That is, welcome it wholeheartedly and receive it! "Repent therefore and be converted, that your sins may be wiped out, so that times of refreshing may come from the presence of the Lord" (Acts 3:19 NKJV).

Always remember, that regardless of what happens in this life, no matter how depressing the world now appears or how difficult life becomes, a life in Christ has a joyful ending. The rewards of Christ are far better than the rewards of this world as Jesus promised His followers this, "an inheritance which is imperishable and undefiled, and will not fade away, reserved in heaven for you, who are protected by the power of God through faith, for a salvation ready to be revealed in the last time," including the 'crown of Life'" (1 Peter 1:4-5 NASB; Rev. 2:10

NASB). Don't reject Christ and make the mistake you'll regret for all eternity. Please, don't miss out on such a great God given opportunity. He has demonstrated His true love for you. (John 3:16 NASB). Who else has ever done so much and offered you so much? He says: Keep watch and be ready, for "this is the last hour, …and many of Christ's enemies have *already* appeared. So we know that the last hour is here" (1John 2:18 CEV). "Yet even now, declares the Lord, return to Me with all your heart" (Joel 2:12 NASB).

CHAPTER 42

Get Ready! What Divine Message Is God Leaving Us?

"I'll put it as urgently as I can: You must get along with each other. You must learn to be considerate of one another, cultivating a life in common" (1 Cor. 1:10 MSG). "God spoke all these words saying; I am the Lord your God, You Shall Have No Other Gods Before Me. You shall Not Make Unto Me Any Graven Images. You Shall Not Take The Name Of The Lord Your God In Vain. Remember The Sabbath Day, To Keep It Holy. Honor Your Father And Mother. You Shall Not Kill. You Shall Not Commit Adultery. You Shall Not Steal. You Shall Not Bear False Witness Against Your Neighbor. You Shall Not Covet" (EX. 20:3-17). "Love one another warmly as Christians, and be eager to show respect for one another" (Rom. 12:10 GNT). "Love is patient and kind. Love is not jealous or boastful or proud or rude. It does not demand its own way. It is not irritable, and it keeps no record of being wronged. It does not rejoice about injustice but rejoices whenever the truth wins out. Love never gives up, never loses faith, is always hopeful, and endures through every circumstance" (1 Corin.13:4-7 NLT). "Our love for each other *proves* that we have gone from death to life. But if you don't love each other, you are still under the power of death" (1 John 3:14 CEV). "Do not judge, and you will not be judged. Do not condemn, and you will not be condemned. Forgive, and you will be forgiven" (Luke 6:37, NIV). "Make allowance for each other's faults, and forgive anyone who offends you. Remember, the Lord forgave you, so you must forgive others" (Col. 3:13 NLT). "But I say to you, Love your enemies, bless them that curse you, do good to them that hate you, and pray for them which despitefully use you and persecute you" (Matt. 5:44 KJV). "So, as those who have been chosen of God, holy and beloved, put on a heart of compassion, kindness, humility, gentleness and patience" (Col. 3:12 NASB). "Put into practice what you learned and received from me" (Phil. 4:9 GNT). "So don't lose a minute in building on what you've been given, complementing your basic faith with good character, spiritual understanding, alert discipline, passionate patience, reverent wonder, warm friendliness, and generous love" (2 Peter 1:5-7 MSG).

"Use every chance you have for doing good" (Eph. 5:16 NCV). "Do not store up for yourselves treasures on earth, where moth and rust destroy, and where thieves break in and steal. But store up for yourselves treasures in heaven, where neither moth nor rust destroys, and where thieves do not break in or steal; for where your treasure is, there your heart will be also" (Matt. 6:19-21 NASB). "And you must love the Lord your God with all your heart, all your soul, and all your strength. And you must commit yourselves wholeheartedly to these commandments that I am giving you today. Repeat them again and again to your children. Talk about them when you are at home and when you are on the road, when you are going to bed and when you are getting up" (Deut. 6:5-7 NLV). "The one who looks intently at the perfect law, and abides by it, not having become a forgetful hearer but an effectual doer, this man shall be blessed in what he does" (James 1:25 NASB).

"The Lord has told you what is good; He has told you what He wants from you: to do what is right to other people, love being kind to others, and live humbly, obeying your God" (Micah 6:8 NCV).

"So get rid of your old self, which made you live as you used to, the old self that was being destroyed by its deceitful desires. Your hearts and minds must be made completely new, and you must put on the new self, which is created in God's likeness and reveals itself in the true life that is upright and holy. No more lying, then! Each of you must tell the truth to the other believer, because we are all members together in the body of Christ. If you become angry, do not let your anger lead you into sin, and do not stay angry all day. Don't give the Devil a chance" (Eph. 4:22-27 GNT).

"Anyone who listens to My teachings and follows it is wise" (Matt. 7:24 NLT). "To those who listen to My teachings, more understanding will be given. But for those who are not listening, even what little understanding they may have will be taken away from them" (Mark 4:25 NLT). "But anyone who hears My teaching and doesn't obey it is foolish" (Matt. 7:26 NLT). Jesus said, "Everyone on the side of truth listens to Me" (John 18:37 NIV). So "Heed instruction and be wise." (Prov. 8:33 NASB). As Jesus said to Thomas, "Stop doubting and believe!" (John 20:27 NIV). "For I am the Lord your God, who takes hold of your right hand and says to you, Do not fear; I will help you" (Isaiah 41:13 NIV). "Devote yourselves to prayer, being watchful and thankful" (Col.4:2 NIV).

"Truly, truly, I say to you, he who believes in Me, has eternal life" (John 6:47 NASB). "But he who does not obey the Son will not see life, but the wrath of God abides on him" (John 3:36 NASB). "Remain in Me, and I will remain in you" (John 15:4 NLT). "For he who finds Me finds life" (Prov. 8:35 NASB). "And behold, I am coming quickly. Blessed is he who heeds the words of the prophecy of this book [the holy Bible]" (Rev. 22:7 NASB). "Whoever believes in Me, as the Scriptures has said, out of his heart will flow rivers of living water" (John 7:38 ESV).

Dear friend, please take a moment to consider the implication of God's words here. Do you understand that our loving creator is telling us over and over, in the clearest possible language, that all true and faithful believers who repent of their sins have an *absolute certainty of salvation*. He says, "Truly, truly, I say to you, he who hears My word, and believes Him who sent Me, has eternal life, and does not come into judgement, but has passed out of death into life" (John 5:24 NASB). "Believe on the Lord Jesus Christ, and thou shalt be saved" (Acts 16:31 AKJV). There is no "if", "but" or "maybe," you will be saved, and "to *obtain* an inheritance which is imperishable and undefiled, and will not fade away, reserved in Heaven for you" (1 Peter 1:4-5 NASB).

"In this, you [should] greatly rejoice, even though now for a little while, if necessary, you have been distressed by various trials" (1 Peter 1:6 NASB). How infinitely grateful we should be for "obtaining as the outcome of our faith the salvation of our souls" (1 Peter 1:9). "Finally, believers, whatever is true, whatever is honorable *and* worthy of respect, whatever is right *and* confirmed by God's word, whatever is pure *and* wholesome, whatever is lovely *and* brings peace, whatever is admirable *and* of good repute; if there is anything worthy of praise, think continually on *these* things [center your mind on them, and implant them in your heart]" (Philip.4:8 AMP).

"The time is fulfilled, and the Kingdom of God is at hand; repent and believe in the gospel" (Mark 1:15 NASB). "Behold, I am coming quickly, and My reward is with Me, to render to every man according to what he has done" (Rev. 22:12 NASB). "I am the Alpha and the Omega, says the Lord God, who is and who was and who is to come, the Almighty" (Rev. 1:8 NASB). "Yes, I am coming quickly, Amen" (Rev. 22:20 NASB).

Comment: The Bible tells us that Jesus will return again. He is not coming as a loving Savior as before. This time He will be coming as a judge, and He will repay every man according to his deeds (see Matt. 16:27). Question: If He were to come tonight or if we were called home tonight, would we be ready for Him? God deeply loves us and is conveying a message of *urgency*, a message of time running out, and a message to quickly turn to our Lord. He is *pleading* that we come to know Him and know His will, and giving warning about an impending judgment if we don't repent. "Turn to Me and be saved, all the ends of the earth! For I am God, and there is no other" (Isa. 45:22 ESV). Do you see how kind and tolerant and patient our God is with us? But just as in the days of Noah before the flood, time is again truly running out for mankind. Not only time, but grace and mercy also.

Before you were born, God planned this moment in your life and it is no accident that you are reading this message today. He is speaking to *you,* and wants a closer relationship with you! In all God's dealings with us, the promises and the conditions are inseparable. If we sincerely fulfill the conditions, God fulfills His promises to us. God will not force His will on you. You are free to choose. However, just for a moment, think of how tenderly God respects your rights and the rights of others, never forcing upon anyone His love and help and salvation. As Scripture says in Isaiah 30:18 NASB, "The Lord *longs* to be gracious to you, and therefore He waits on high to have compassion on you." God's loving arms have not been shortened but are still stretched out, still longing and waiting to be allowed to help, to reach out, to save, to bless, and to answer you.

Know that God expressed His willingness to make an agreement with you, to make a promise, a covenant with you and it bears His signature in the death and resurrection of His Son Jesus Christ. Want to know what that promise is? "Draw near to God and He *will* draw near to you" (James 4:8 ESV). The moment you faithfully comply with His written Word and become personally involved in the agreement to draw near to God, from that very moment the entire promise and covenant from God is in force towards *you.* Don't lose hold of this promise. Know, as we see in Revelation 12:9, that Satan is the one deceiving the whole world. Don't let him deceive you!

Recognize that the first step in satanic deception is sowing seeds of doubt in a person's mind about God's Word, and suggesting different interpretations and attempting to invalidate part or all of the Bible. The more you know the Word, the *better* you are protected. The one ingredient a person must have to believe and be saved is God's Word! For this very reason, it is the one ingredient that Satan wants to take away from you! If he fails to take it away, life results, and as Jesus said to those who believed Him, "If you continue in My word, *then* you are truly disciples of Mine, and you will know the truth, and the truth will make you free" (John 8:31-32 NASB). But . . .

Free from what, you ask? Free from Satan's binding power of deception and the heavy chains of spiritual death. The evil one abhors your closeness to God and the Bible, and his demonic underlings are determined to destroy our intimacy, discredit our God, and induce our thoughts of not reading the Bible. Do not be misled. You are engaged in massive warfare, spiritually speaking. The best defense against Satan's warfare and his underlings is knowing God's word. We must therefore drench ourselves and saturate ourselves daily with His Word. Just as you cannot expect to wash a full load of dishes or laundry with just a trickle drip of water, likewise, you cannot expect just a Sunday trickle of God's Word will suffice. We need follow our Lord's instruction book and abide in His Word and do as He commands in Joshua 1:8 that says, "This book of the law shall not depart from your mouth, but you shall meditate on it day and night, so that you may be careful to do according to all that is written in it;" And God promises us this, "He who believes in Me… out of his heart will flow rivers of living water" (John 7:38 NKJV).

Remember, reading and interpreting Scripture is about drawing the meaning out of the Bible, not putting a meaning onto the verses. Read Galatians 1:8-9 to see what Scripture says of those who preach something different from the true gospel of Jesus Christ. Be very careful of negative influences and those that discredit any part of Christ's statements or authority.

Scripture affirms, "Believe in the Lord Jesus, and you shall be saved" (Acts 16:31 NASB). "Trust in the Lord with all your heart and do not lean on your own understanding. In all your ways acknowledge Him, and He will make your paths straight" (Prov. 3:5-6 NASB). Do not let any person or religion steer you away from your trust and allegiance to Christ. Rather, quietly bless them and pray for them. They are not your enemy! Satan the great deceiver is. Scripture says, "For our struggle is not against flesh and blood, but against the rulers, against the authorities, against the powers of this dark world and against the spiritual forces of evil in the heavenly realms" (Eph. 6:12 NIV). Be wise therefore to seek out and "link up" in godly fellowship with those who fully trust and preach the Word of God and truly have a heart to spiritually help, uplift, and encourage you. Never let go of Christ.

This world is not our home; we are looking forward to our everlasting home in heaven. Measured against eternity, your time on this earth is but a blink of an eye, but the consequences of it will last forever. The deeds of this life are the destiny of the next. We should be realizing that every moment we spend in these earthly bodies is time spent away from our eternal home in heaven with Jesus.

Know that eternal life in heaven can be yours today, if you sincerely believe in Jesus Christ and all He claimed to be. If you are reading this and understand this, God is *calling on you*. Will He choose you now? That depends on what *you* do. If you act on the knowledge God is revealing to you, He will communicate *more* understanding. The more we act and abide and believe, the more He reveals. But remember, "We please God by what we *do*, and not only by what we believe" (James 2:24 CEV). Jesus is at your door knocking! Please, will you let Him in? He says to you in Scripture, "Look! I have been standing at the door, and I am constantly knocking. If anyone hears me calling him and opens the door, I will come in and fellowship with him and he with Me" (Rev. 3:20 TLB). Know that He's at *your door knocking*, please, receive and welcome Him!

God's Decree: "But to all who receive *and* welcome Him, He gave the right [the authority, the privilege] to become children of God, *that is*, to those who believe in (adhere to, trust in, and rely on) His name" (John 1:12 AMP). "And you also were included in Christ when you heard the message of truth, the gospel of your salvation. When you *believed*, you were marked in Him with a Seal, the promised Holy Spirit, who is a deposit *guaranteeing our inheritance* until the redemption of those who are

God's possession, to the praise of His glory" (Eph. 1:13-14 NIV). Oh dear friend, please stop here and take a moment to consider His words, His wonderful promises, and how great our Lord is and the debt of gratitude we truly owe Him. In everything and every way we need be thankful to Him.

Know that Christ's body of believers desires that this handbook will become a tool to acquaint you with God's great plan and enhance your present understanding of the Bible. We pray this book containing God's profound and urgent message will stimulate you to a lifetime of discovering for yourself the amazing truths and magnificent promises presented in God's Word, the Holy Bible. It is a divine book that has changed the world and carries both the Word and the promises of God. The Bible has been historically recognized as the most important book for the development of both the rule of law and the democratic institutions in the Western world. No other religion, teaching, nation or movement has so changed the world for the better as Christianity has done.

There is absolutely nothing of greater value that can provide eternal benefits and that compares to the wisdom found in God's miraculous book called the Bible. Christianity is based on the Bible, God's Word. Through it we are able to discover and learn what our Creator has planned for us and how He made provision for us to spend eternity *with Him*. Christianity is unique in that it is the only faith that states you can do nothing to "earn your way" into heaven. It is only what Jesus did for us that grants entrance into God's eternal kingdom (see Gal. 1:4). We all need to reset our priorities. We need to read the Scriptures repetitiously. Make time for it. Read it. Study it. Believe it and be absorbed by it. Begin reading with the New Testament and persevere in these things, for as you do this, you will ensure salvation.

It will change your life. The most important decision you will ever make on this earth is the decision you make about your eternity. Please, do not postpone it. Do not neglect it! Do it now. For some of us, there may not be a tomorrow! God may call us early. One thing is certain, a time is coming when you will meet Jesus because He is inescapable and unavoidable. And if you do not meet Him as your Savior, you will meet Him as your Judge. It does not matter how you treated Him on this earth. In fact, you may have ignored Him, discredited Him, denied Him and even cursed Him, but one day, you will absolutely stand before Him.

As we conclude the study of all the important Chapter questions in this book, there now remains but one question left. Where do **you** stand in all this? Have you accepted God's greatest witness and the testimony of our Lord and Savior Jesus Christ? Remember: It is because of Him that we can say we may never experience hell, but eternal life in heaven. Eternal life is available to all those who choose to put their faith and trust in Him. In Acts 16:31 the Bible affirms, "Believe in the Lord Jesus and you will be saved." It is our prayer that you receive the greatest gift of all, abundant life... eternal life in Jesus Christ. By receiving the free gift of salvation through Jesus, by giving your life to Him, you can be granted a new life with purpose you never before imagined.

In closing, know that we are earnestly praying for you and family, and as Paul, a devoted apostle of Christ, said, "That the God of our Lord Jesus Christ, may give you a Spirit of wisdom and understanding in the knowledge of Him." We pray that when you read God's word the Bible, you accept it not as the word of men, but for what it really is, the Word of God, which also performs its "work" in all those who *believe*.

We pray that the eyes of your heart may be enlightened, so that you may know what is the hope of His calling, what are the riches of the glory of His inheritance, and what is the surpassing greatness of His power toward those who *believe*. "In all your ways acknowledge Him, and He shall direct your paths" (Prov. 3:6 KJV). What a wonderful promise! Jesus said, "Be faithful until death, and I will give you the Crown of Life!" (Rev. 2:10 NASB). Oh, the blessings of God that will come to you if you learn to believe and trust in Christ.

Part 8

Scriptural Summary Points to Remember

- The Bible is God's divine book and loving message for our guidance, our instruction, and our salvation. No other book receives His endorsement.

- It is as declared "The pure and inerrant Word of God in all its parts." Any religion or preacher that thinks differently and adds to, subtracts from, or distorts any part of the Bible does not represent our God of the Bible.

- There is only one faith, one body of believers, and one God for all of us.

- Learn to recognize perverse teachings.

- Any religion teaching something different from the gospel of Christ and the Bible is a religion that does *not* represent God. Turn away from them.

- Do not be carried away by varied and strange teachings. God said, "We have the Prophetic Word, *made more sure*, to which you do well to pay attention" (2 Peter 1:19 NASB).

- There are grave and eternal consequences for the nonbeliever, and as Scripture warns: "The wrath of God abides on him."

- God created you and knows *everything* about you and cares dearly for you.

- He loves you as much as His own Son and wants you in heaven with Him.

- He is *pleading* for your attention, "Listen to Me, trust in Me, abide in Me."

- Yet even now, declares the Lord, "Return to Me with all your heart."

- "Whosoever transgresseth, and abideth *not* in the doctrine of Christ, hath *not* God. He that abideth in the doctrine of Christ, he hath both the Father and the Son" (2 John 9 KJV).

- Time and grace and mercy are *quickly* running out; reset your priorities now!

- There is a hell to shun and a heaven to gain. Therefore, repent and believe in the gospel of Christ. Why?

- Because born-again Christian believers are to obtain an inheritance which is imperishable and undefiled and will not fade away, reserved in heaven for *you*.

- O Nations of the earth, listen to Me. Abide in Me. Turn to Me and be saved, all the ends of the earth; for I am God, there is no other.

- "Behold, I am coming quickly. Put into practice what you learned and received. Do not fear; I will help you. Truly, truly, I say to you, he who believes in Me, has eternal life."

CHAPTER 43

A Special Word From Our Heavenly Father

My dear child,

I know everything about you...(Psalms 139:1). I am your creator. You were in My care even before you were born...(Isaiah 44:2). I know when you sit down and when you rise up...(Psalms 139:2). I am familiar with all your ways...(Psalms 139:3). Even the very hairs on your head are numbered...(Matthew 10:30). For you were made in My image...(Genesis 1:27). For in Me you live and move and exist and have your being...(Acts 17:28). For you are My offspring...(Acts 17:28). Before I formed you in the womb I knew you... (Jeremiah 1:5). You were predestined before I planned creation...(Ephesians 1:10-11). You were not a mistake... (Psalms 139:15:16).

For all your days are written in My Book...(Psalms 139:15-16). I determined the exact time of your birth and where you would live... (Acts 17:26). You are fearfully and wonderfully made...(Psalms 139:14). I weaved you together in your mother's womb...(Psalms 139:13). And brought you forth and sustained you from birth...(Psalms 71:6).

I have been misrepresented by those who don't know me...(John 8:41-44). *I am not distant and angry, but am the complete expression of love...*(1John 4:16). *And it is My desire to lavish My love on you, simply because you are My child and I am your Father...*(1John 3:1). *I love you more than your earthly father ever could...*(Matthew 7:11). *For I am the perfect Father...*(Matthew 5:48).

Every good gift that you received comes from My hand...(James 1:17). *For I am your provider and I will meet your needs...*(Matthew 6:31-33). *For I know the (eternal) plans that I have for you, plans to give you hope and a future...*(Jeremiah 29:11). *Because I love you with an everlasting love...*(Jeremiah 31:3). *My thoughts toward you are as countless as the sands on the seashore...*(Psalms 139:17-18). *And I will rejoice over you with shouts of joy...*(Zephaniah 3:17). *I will never stop doing good for you...*(Jeremiah 32:40).

For you are My treasured possession...(Exodus 19:5). *I desire to establish you with all My heart and all My soul...*(Jeremiah 32:41). *And I want to show you great and mighty things which you do not know...* (Jeremiah 33:3). *If you seek Me with all your heart, you will find Me...*(Deuteronomy 4:29). *Long for the pure milk of the word...[The Bible]* (1Peter 2:2). *Seek from the book of the Lord and read...*(Isaiah 34:16). *Meditate on it day and night...*(Joshua 1:8). *For they are Life to those who find them...*(Proverbs 4:20-22).

Delight in Me, and I will give you the desires of your heart...(Psalms 37:4). *For it is I who gave you those desires...*(Philippians 2:13). *I am able to do more than you could possibly imagine...*(Ephesians 3:20). *For I am your greatest encourager...*(2Thessalonians 2:16-17). *I am also the Father who comforts you in all your troubles...*(2Corinthians 1:3-4). *When you are brokenhearted, I am close to you...*(Psalms 34:18). *As a shepherd carries a lamb, I have carried you close to My heart...*(Isaiah 40:11).

One day I will wipe away every tear from your eyes...(Revelation 21:3-4). And I will take away all the discomfort and pain you have suffered on this earth...(Revelation 21:3-4). I am your Father and I love you even as I love My own Son Jesus...(John 17:23). For in Jesus My love for you is revealed...(John 17:26). He is the exact representation of My being...(Hebrews 1:3). And He came to demonstrate that I am for you, not against you...(Romans...8:31). Therefore, if you are in Christ you are a new creature, and I shall not count your sins... (2Corinthians 5:17-19).

Jesus died so that you and I could be reconciled...(2Corinthians 5:18-19). His death was the ultimate expression of love for you...(1John 4:10). God gave up everything He loved, [His Son] that He might gain your love...(Romans 8:31-32). If you truly believe and receive the gift of My Son Jesus, you receive Me...(1 John 2:23). And nothing will ever separate you from My love again...(Romans 8:38-39).

To you it has been given to know the mystery of the kingdom of God...(Mark 4:11). By My divine power I have granted you everything pertaining to life and godliness, I have granted you precious and magnificent promises in order that you might become partakers of the divine nature. Now for this reason, apply all diligence and add to your faith virtue, and to virtue knowledge, and to knowledge temperance, and to temperance patience, and to patience godliness, and to godliness brotherly kindness, and to kindness love. For if you practice these things and they are increasing you shall not fall;

For in this way, the entrance into the Eternal Kingdom of our Lord and Savior Jesus Christ will be abundantly supplied to you... (2Peter 1:3-11). To obtain an inheritance which is imperishable and undefiled and will not fade away, reserved in Heaven for you, who are protected by the power of God through faith for a salvation ready to be revealed in the end of time...(1Peter 1:4-5). Repent therefore and be converted that your sins may be blotted out...(Acts 3:19). Give attention to reading of Scripture... be absorbed in them. Pay close attention... Persevere in these things for as you do this you will ensure salvation both for yourself and for those who hear you...(1Tim. 4:13, 15-16). Do not be carried away by varied and strange teachings...(Hebrew 13:9). Put into practice what you've learned and received from Me...(Phil. 4:9). Don't lose a minute in building on what you've been given... (2Peter 1:5-7). Listen to Me... Heed instruction and be wise, for he who finds Me finds Life...(Proverbs 8:32-35).

Truly, truly, I say to you, he who hears My Word, and believes Him who sent Me, has Eternal Life, and does not come into condemnation, but has passed out of death into life...(John 5:24). He who has the Son has life; he who does not have the Son does not have life. These things I have written to you who believe in the name of the Son of God, in order that you may know that you have eternal life...(1John 5:12-13). Behold, I am coming quickly... (Rev. 3:11). It is the last hour...(1John 2:18). Look for the blessed hope and the glorious appearing of the great God and Savior Jesus Christ... (Titus 2:13). Watch for My return!.. (Mark 13:37). I will never leave you nor forsake you...(Hebrews 13:5). With Eternal Love,

Your Heavenly Father,

I am the Alpha and the Omega, who is and who was and who is to come, (Revelation.1:8)

The Lord Almighty

CHAPTER 44

A Prayer to Express One's Heart's Desire to Seek the Lord

O dear heavenly Father, thank You for loving me in spite of all my sins, and thank You for the free gift of eternal life. I'm sorry for my past sins and ask You to forgive me. Jesus, I believe You died on the cross for my sins and arose from the dead. You paid for my sins with Your precious blood and I believe it. I turn away from my sins and repent, and I open the door of my heart and invite You to come into my life. I place my complete trust in You alone for eternal life, and ask that You help me become the person You want me to be. Thank You, Lord, for saving me. In Jesus' name I pray, Amen.

Note from the Author

Bring Blessings
Help People!!
Share the Good News
Spread the Book
And Save Souls

I give you this charge: Share the Word; be prepared in season and out of season; correct, rebuke and encourage, with great patience and careful instruction (2 Tim.4:1-2). Not to force people to *want* to be saved, but to shine God's light and share our faith with those who *do*.

Sharing God's word of how people can have Eternal Life is the greatest thing you can ever do for them. If you think you are too important to help someone, you are only fooling yourself. Gal 6:3

Jesus said; You shall be my witnesses... Acts 1:8
We are Christ's Ambassadors and representatives... 2 Corinthians 5:20
Go everywhere in the world, and tell them the Good News... Mk 16:15
We all need Jesus. He is the *only* one who can save people. Acts 4:12

And whatever you do for the least of these brothers
and sisters of Mine, you do for Me. Matthew 25:40, NIV
And if you give even a cup of cold water to one of the least of
My followers, you will *surely* be rewarded. Matthew 10:42, NLT

Therefore, your mission has *very great and eternal significance.*
Absolutely nothing else you do will ever matter as much as
Praying and helping people establish an eternal relationship with God.

Order Information

To order additional copies of this book, please visit
www.redemption-press.com.

This book is also available as an e-book

Also available on Amazon.com and BarnesandNoble.com
Or by calling toll free 1-844-2REDEEM.